Business
Portfolio
Management

Wiley Financial Management Series

The Valuation of Information Technology: A Guide for Strategy Development, Valuation, and Financial Planning, by Christopher Gardner

Business Portfolio Management: Valuation, Risk Assessment, and EVA™ Strategies, by Michael S. Allen

Business
Portfolio
Management

Wiley Financial Management Series

The Valuation of Information Technology: A Guide for Strategy Development, Valuation, and Financial Planning, by Christopher Gardner

Business Portfolio Management: Valuation, Risk Assessment, and EVA™ Strategies, by Michael S. Allen

Business Portfolio Management

Valuation, Risk Assessment, and EVA™ Strategies

Michael S. Allen

John Wiley & Sons, Inc.

New York • Chichester • Weinheim
Brisbane • Singapore • Toronto

Published by John Wiley & Sons, Inc.

Published simultaneously in Canada.

Library of Congress Cataloging-in-Publication Data:

Allen, Michael S., 1942 –
    Business portfolio management : valutation, risk assessment, and EVA™ strategies /
Michael S. Allen.
        p.   cm. — (Wiley financial management series)
        Includes index.
        ISBN 0-471-37640-X (cloth : alk. paper)
        1. Portfolio management.   2. Stockholders.   3. Strategic planning.
I. Title.   II. Series.

HG4529.5 .A44 2000
658.15′2 — dc21

                                                            99-046189

Printed in the United States of America.

10   9   8   7   6   5   4   3   2   1

Contents

Preface

The main responsibility of executives is to optimize the value of their businesses. To do so, they must find, develop, and pursue the best possible strategies and allocate limited resources to their most productive uses. These are challenging tasks for executives of any company—in any industry—but even more challenging when the company is a portfolio of multiple subsidiaries, divisions, strategic business units, or products. The level of difficulty seems to rise exponentially with the number of units in the portfolio. This difficulty may explain why I and my colleagues at Navigant Consulting, through decades of experience, have failed to find a portfolio company operating anywhere *near* its full value potential.

This book aims to assist executives and staff who are eager to tap value-creating portfolio concepts and practical tools they can apply today to achieve success. In the chapters that follow, readers will learn, among other things, how to objectively measure the economic efficiency of an existing business portfolio and its constituent units, how to assess the risk of current and prospective strategies, how to bring to the table alternatives with greater value, and how to apply a life-cycle view of the value-creating potency of different portfolio units. Perhaps as important, readers will be introduced to an objective process for finding, evaluating, and choosing among different strategic alternatives. Members of the financial analysis community will also find these perspectives on corporate value creation highly useful.

Acknowledgments

Many people contributed to this book, particularly my colleagues at Navigant Consulting, who helped develop the intellectual framework of its portfolio strategy practice. Special recognition must go to Carl Spetzler, who developed two essential concepts used throughout the book: the *success template* in the 1980s and, in collaboration with Paul Skov, the *dialogue decision process* in the late 1970s. Vince Barabba of General Motors coined the name of this process within one of the world's largest enterprises.

Richard Luecke of Salem, Massachusetts, provided invaluable assistance in writing this book, and my colleagues at Navigant made numerous suggestions for its improvement. The comments of David Matheson and Ed Scheuer were particularly helpful. Stephen Malinak was very helpful in disguising examples.

I thank my family, who supported me and endured months of lost weekends while the manuscript was in development.

Finally, I would like to thank my clients who over the past 30 years have contributed to my understanding of how corporations build or destroy value.

Michael Allen
Menlo Park, California

1

How Portfolios Build Value

Much has been written over the past few years about the growing importance and influence of virtual corporations, of networks of collaborating organizations, of strategic partnerships, and of competition between opposing supply chains. It is difficult to find a major enterprise that is not currently involved in one or more of these relationships, and there is every reason to believe that these relationships will command an even greater share of economic activity in the years ahead.

Nevertheless, the main engines of economic activity in North America and around the globe continue to be individual corporations, many of which organize around portfolios of business units. General Electric, Coca-Cola, Procter & Gamble, Hewlett-Packard, Motorola, Citigroup, Merck, Pfizer, and Lockheed Martin represent just a handful of today's great portfolio companies, and all owe their growth and prosperity to the dynamism of their portfolio units. Unlike portfolio companies of the past, these corporations maintain focus, often sharing technologies, core competencies, or "success templates" they have learned to manage well. They also recognize the importance of *process* in effective management.

Even the best-managed portfolio companies, however, can do better. More than 30 years of consulting practice has convinced me that most corporations can achieve striking increases in shareholder value through the strategic management of their portfolios of subsidiaries, business units, and product categories. To do so, however, they need to do a better job of the following:

- Creating real strategic alternatives.
- Accurately estimating the value of those alternatives.
- Understanding the risks involved in each alternative.

Once those tasks are accomplished, decision makers still need a reliable framework for choosing between alternatives, for making trade-offs between risks and opportunities, and for understanding how the individual units of their portfolios will interact. Fortunately, the discipline of financial economics has created such a framework, one that any diligent non–financial manager can borrow and apply. This book describes that framework and offers practical techniques that have helped dozens of companies increase the value of their business portfolios.

THE CHECKERED PAST
OF PORTFOLIO COMPANIES

Despite the success of the portfolio companies mentioned previously, portfolio companies are not generally held in high repute, and the reason lies in the conglomerate era of the 1960s and 1970s. Any book that claims to offer a better way of creating value in portfolio companies must revisit that era, if only to underscore what *not* to do.

Portfolio businesses were all the rage in the 1960s and early 1970s. Investors eagerly snapped up shares of conglomerates like ITT, LTV, Textron, Gulf & Western, and Litton Industries. The idea of growth through aggressive acquisition was intellectually appealing, and it also appeared to produce tangible results. At their peaks, these companies were hot! Investors were paying 20 to 30 times earnings for their shares—60 times current earnings for Litton Industries' stock in 1968. Shareholders were seeing huge increases in value.

Impressed by these results, other corporations turned away from their traditional labors and went fishing for acquisitions in unrelated industries, casting for whatever had the potential to fuel earnings growth and greater share appreciation.

Wall Street loved the conglomerates. The financial engineering that brought them together and the increased share value that resulted were things that Wall Street people understood and appreciated; many, in fact, had played a direct hand in the deal making that had made the conglomerates possible. For example, Lazard Frères & Company's Felix Rohatyn brought a smorgasbord of acquisition candidates to ITT's Harold Geneen during the 1960s. From that varied menu, Geneen selected companies in such disparate fields as air conditioners, industrial pumps, life insurance, car rentals (Avis), taxi service (Yellow Cab of Kansas City), hotels (including Sheraton), parking lots, secretarial-vocational trade schools, book publishing, home building (Levitt of Levittown fame), and even baking (Continental Baking). How these companies fit in with ITT's international telecommunications business was anyone's guess. In 1968 alone, ITT acquired 20 domestic companies. In most cases, ITT's stratospheric stock price made it possible to buy up assets with its own shares and a modest amount of cash.

Expanding shareholder wealth through conglomeration had nothing to do with management and everything to do with the numbers and with the financial alchemy that raised the market multiples of conglomerate companies to remarkable levels. Price-earning (P-E) ratios soared as giants like ITT swallowed up more and more smaller companies.

But didn't all this feeding simply give the conglomerate company a bad case of indigestion? What, after all, did ITT's executives know about the baking industry or about running a taxicab company? What did Gulf & Western know about the publishing business when it acquired Simon & Schuster? What did Litton executives know about creating economic development on the island of Crete and mainland Greece, a project they undertook with great fanfare in 1967? Absolutely nothing, except, perhaps, that "business is business."

Conglomerators believed that good managers could manage anything. And sometimes that is indeed true. Conglomerate king Harold Geneen was one of the few who could do so, within limits. As business historian Robert Sobel describes him, "Geneen was confident to the point of arrogance about his ability to manage an enterprise—any one, in virtually any industry."[1] An accountant by training, Geneen relied heavily on financial data to control his far-flung empire. He was assisted in this by a central staff of some 400 administrative, technical, and financial experts who acted as his fact finders and fact checkers. The system was designed to pick up signals of trouble and head them off quickly. If sales were seen to lag, unit managers followed a two-step company drill: first, cut costs; second, attempt to boost sales.[2]

Geneen immersed himself in the numbers of his wide-ranging businesses and used his mastery of those numbers to control his general managers. Every month, ITT's 50 top managers convened with the master in a closed conference room high atop the company's New York City headquarters. Everyone would have before them a six-inch thick book with the words "ITT, General Management Meeting, System Confidential" stamped boldly in gold lettering. Between the covers of this tome were all the facts and financials of ITT's operating units. During the course of several days of meetings, Geneen would alternatively grill and chastise his executives, asking why certain results had fallen short and what the executive planned to do about it. These meetings sometimes ran for 16 hours at a stretch.

Similar meetings at lower levels shadowed these top-level monthly meetings. In addition, Geneen expected each unit to develop and present an annual budget and annual strategic plan. Meetings, reports, plans, data collection, and constant checking kept him informed and in control of his empire. Or so it appeared.

Many began to see the portfolio company as a form of corporate mutual fund. In this metaphor, a company with many operating units was like mutual-fund portfolio, with the chief executive officer (CEO) as portfolio manager. Assembling a portfolio of units with highly volatile but weakly correlated returns (earnings) would theoretically achieve the same return with lower earnings volatility (risk).

The corporation-as-mutual-fund idea aimed to reduce risk through diversification, optimize portfolio results at a given level of risk, and create greater total portfolio returns through judicious buying and selling. No intervention into the internal operations of these portfolio companies was required by the manager, except to cajole and put unit managers through annual hell weeks in order to get better results. After all, mutual-fund managers didn't try to run the companies in their portfolios. They didn't sit on their boards or deal with their personnel; they didn't work with them to identify and select alternative paths to future growth. It wasn't necessary. If an operating unit failed to perform as anticipated, the CEO–investment manager could simply sell the unit and replace it with something else.

Simply having a portfolio of businesses, however, did not guarantee continued economic success. Indeed, most of the conglomerate highfliers of yesteryear eventually went into steep dives. These firms sank because they rarely added value to the portfolio units. As Michael Porter has noted, "Diversified companies do not compete; only their business units do. Unless a corporate strategy places primary attention on nurturing the success of each unit, the strategy will fail."[3] Such nurturing of portfolio units is precisely what the big conglomerates failed to do. They were unable to identify, fund, and encourage growth opportunities within their portfolio units.

Once the inflow of new earnings gained through acquisitions ended, so did the earnings growth of the conglomerates.

Conglomerate companies were not entirely bad or wrongheaded. Some provided financial management and control systems that most of their newly acquired units had previously lacked. Budget and management accounting techniques developed in the automobile industry, for example, were adopted by companies like ITT and their various business units, where they did much good. However, once these systems were in place, conglomerate managers had little else to contribute except expensive overhead. Years later, Jack Welch described these stifling overheads, which plagued his own company, General Electric: "Headquarters can...strangle, choke, delay, and create insecurity.... We don't need the questioners and the checkers, the nit-pickers who bog down the process, people whose only role is to second-guess people and clog communications inside the company.... Each staff person has to ask 'How do I add value? How do I help make people on the line more effective and more competitive?'"[4] Even worse, financial controls were often used to kill whatever growth opportunities may have sprouted in the portfolio units.

Like the mutual-fund managers whose behavior they mirrored, the conglomerate managers pressured their unit managers for continuous improvements in quarterly earnings. They treated every business with the same annual strategic planning process, whether it was a developing enterprise, explosively growing, or a mature business. This pressure naturally encouraged near-term earnings growth at the expense of the long-term and risky initiatives on which innovation and industry-altering breakthroughs depend.

There was also not much strategic sense in how the conglomerate CEOs created their empires. Despite much wishful thinking and bold predictions of interunit synergies, acquisitions were generally motivated by the desire to purchase a stream of future earnings from current businesses. The concept of *success template* and the related notions of shared technologies and competencies were often missed entirely. Consider the case of ITT, the king of the conglomerates. It was already positioned dead center in telecommunications, which was becoming one of the most explosive growth industries of the postwar era. More promising still, it had footholds in the non-U.S. markets where effective telecommunications systems would be in the greatest demand, and where economic growth was poised to take off. As for competition, it would have been natural for the developing countries to turn to ITT for effective communications systems in the 1960s. Telecommunications was one of the things that Americans did better than anyone. But instead of seeking ways to exploit its own huge growth possibilities, ITT executives busied themselves with staking out positions in domestic companies that made Twinkies, sold fire insurance, ran parking lots, and rented hotel rooms.[5]

PORTFOLIO MANAGEMENT IN THE POSTCONGLOMERATE ERA

By the early 1970s, Wall Street's fascination with big conglomerates had evaporated, and the theories that supported confidence in corporate portfolio strategy were quickly turned on their heads and replaced with mirror-opposite theories. The idea that good managers could manage anything fell out of favor—a few notable exceptions notwithstanding. A new theory instructed corporate strategists to "stick to their knitting"—that is, to stay in the businesses they understood and to stop creating portfolios of unrelated and mismatched companies and initiatives. Stick-to-your-knitting advocates had this message for senior executives:

> Everything we've told you about portfolio management, risk management, asset selection, and divestiture remains true. However, if a shareholder wants to buy a mutual fund, he'll talk to his broker. Thousands are available, and all have management fees that are much lower than yours. It is more efficient for the shareholder-investor to assemble a portfolio through the open market than for you to attempt the same through an expensive and problematic process of acquisitions.
>
> So instead of playing mutual-fund manager, focus your business in the areas you can best manage for future profits and growth. In a word, companies serve investors best when they are "pure plays"—that is, when they are focused within a single line of business.

Despite the appealing logic of the pure-play theory, many of the greatest names in corporate America today are *not* pure plays but portfolios of businesses. Others that were burned during the conglomerate years divested themselves of many holdings but remain strong and effective portfolio companies. Obviously, someone knows how to do this right. There is plenty of evidence that corporations *can* create value through portfolios if they act as astute managers and add more benefits than costs to the mix. Good portfolio managers encourage internal growth, enforce financial discipline, reduce total overhead, reduce the cost of capital to their units, allow units to take greater risks than they could as stand-alone businesses, and even provide opportunities for synergy and for technology sharing.

A pure play is not best for the individual investor, nor is the investor the only party whose needs must be satisfied by the business manager. There are other stakeholders. Employees and managers want to work for companies that can renew themselves, survive, and prosper over time. Many pure-play companies have no future in a fast-changing world; they are doomed to extinction as their products and services become obsolete or go out of fashion, forcing their employees and managers to either abandon ship or go down with it.

Portfolios represent a bridge to the future, satisfying a universal emotional need among shareholders, employees, and host communities to be part of a dynamic, healthy, and growing enterprise, one that provides security, rewards, and a place near the leading edge of progress. Lacking this bridge, companies cannot attract and retain good employees. Where would Hewlett-Packard (HP) and its employees be today if it had stuck to its knitting as a test-and-measurement instrument company? Today, HP's printer operation alone is large enough to rank among the Fortune 500 companies, and the test and measurement unit is being spun off. Its personal computer division is one of the world's leading producers. Would Corning exist today if it had not ventured beyond its once powerful products: light bulbs and later, television tubes? Although those businesses have virtually evaporated in North America, Corning has replaced them—in spades—with new and profitable ventures in fiber optics, the materials found in catalytic converters, and other high-end products. And today, General Electric shareholders profit immensely from businesses that its early founders never envisioned. Fortunately for their employees *and* their investors, these companies created vibrant portfolios of new products and services even as their original businesses have withered away.

GOOD ALTERNATIVES ARE THE KEY

The seeking, evaluation, and selection of the most-promising alternatives are at the heart of this book. One could postulate that all great value creation is found in good alternatives. The experience of General Electric (GE) underscores this point. This company could have continued to be a major player in the consumer-electronics business. With its acquisition of RCA in 1986, it had the product lines, manufacturing, and distribution to slug it out with the Asian producers that dominated the field. But consumer electronics, excepting a few product categories, was becoming a glutted, low-margin commodity business, and GE's consumer-electronics business was already losing $125 million a year. Sensing that the battle for the consumer-products market would be either too costly or unwinnable, the company found and pursued alternatives in medical imaging, consumer and commercial finance, aircraft engines, and other more promising areas. It sold its consumer electronics business in the late 1980s to France's Thomson Group in return for cash and Thomson's high-tech medical imaging business, which was generating over $1 billion in sales. This trade strengthened GE's already-strong position in the medical-systems business. Today, its shareholders and employees are reaping the benefits of those alternatives.

Corning, too, probably could have held its grip on the television-tube business it initially dominated. In the early days of television, the television-tube business was, in the words of one Corning executive, "raining money."[6] But television-tube making was becoming a mature business with slower growth and lower margins—and plenty of offshore competition. Fortunately for its stakeholders, Corning had worked for years on developing alternatives in the fields of fiber optics and specialized ceramic materials.

Both GE and Corning went on to create much more value for their shareholders, and their diligence in seeking superior alternatives was key to their success. Creating and capitalizing on alternatives, however, requires two important things:

1. A *culture* that encourages people to seek out high-value alternatives.
2. A *process* that executives and employees can use to determine which alternatives are best, and how they can be most effectively pursued.

Both concepts are addressed in Chapter 2. Subsequent chapters will explain practical methods for implementing the alternative-seeking process. Of the two, culture may be the most important. Executives universally pontificate on the need for new ideas and the virtues of risk taking. It is in the shareholders' interest for managers to take calculated risks when opportunities present themselves. Risk taking is the first and most essential step in all human progress. But how many companies actually encourage that sentiment or support it with incentives? Risk taking may be verbally encouraged, but in most firms the burden of risk is borne by individual employees, who cannot afford to bear it, and not by the organization, which can. And so many opportunities are left on the table.

The failure of organizations to deal effectively with risk practically guarantees that the alternatives capable of invigorating their businesses will not be found. This is because alternatives represent risky, unexplored territory, and people who don't know how to define and measure risk—or even discuss it—will avoid risky alternatives in favor of the known world of products, services, and firm capabilities. The inability to deal with risk suggests, perhaps, why a financially trained person like ITT's Harold Geneen was so disinclined to pursue the murky but dynamic future of telecommunications and so keen to acquire mundane companies whose future earning streams were more visible and predictable.

TOWARD EFFICIENT PORTFOLIOS

Perhaps the biggest mistake of the 1960s conglomerates was their failure to add value in excess of the overhead they created. Lewis Berman put his finger on this problem when he wrote, "The most damaging result of the conglomerate era was the false legitimacy it seemed to confer on the pursuit of profits from financial manipulation *rather than by producing something of genuine economic value* [emphasis added]."[7] Seeking operating efficiencies is the obvious way to add economic value in excess of overhead cost, but this is usually a one-time fix. More is required. After seeking operating efficiencies, the modern portfolio corporation has three jobs to do. The first is to optimize the trade-offs its units must make. These trade-offs might be risk versus return, increased shareholder value versus short-term earnings, or something else. The second job is to help the operating units grow through the internal development of value-adding alternatives. The third job is to consider acquisitions and divestitures that will strengthen the current portfolio of units. I introduce the first of these jobs here; the others are addressed in subsequent chapters.

To understand the first job of the portfolio manager—optimizing the trade-offs faced by the business units—one needs to understand the idea of the *efficient frontier,* a concept first developed and applied in the field of financial economics. To financial scholars and money managers, the efficient frontier is a curve on a two-dimensional graph representing the relationship between risk and return for a set of portfolios. An investment portfolio is efficient to the extent that it maximizes return for a given level of risk. This same concept, adapted to reflect the relationship between shareholder value and short-term earnings or other important results, can help us in the management of business portfolios.

Here is a brief explanation for readers who have not encountered the efficient-frontier concept elsewhere. Imagine for a moment that we are money managers for a big mutual-fund company. Our job is to create a set of investment portfolios to serve the needs of thousands of different investors. As market pros, nobody has to tell us about the correlation between the returns our investors seek and the risks that must be taken to get them. In their innards, our investors understand the connection between these two factors. Some of our investors—particularly retirees—are highly risk averse. They want a good return on their money but demand safety of principal above all else. They don't want us to take any major risks with their life savings! We know that other client investors are fairly fearless and want us to seek investment opportunities with the greatest long-run returns. And of course, plenty of other investors are between these two poles; they are willing to accept some calculated risks in seeking positive returns on their capital.

Given these diverse customers, we crank up our computers and databases and assemble seven portfolios. Some of these portfolios contain low-risk assets, like treasury bills (T-bills) and bank certificates of deposit (CDs). Others are a diversified mix of corporate bonds and the stocks of dozens of Standard & Poor's 500 companies. Other portfolios are narrowly composed of small emerging companies—or exotic stuff, such as gold-mining companies, biotech companies with big plans but no products in the market, and so forth. Based on past performance and informed hunches—and lots of number crunching—we estimate the risk and expected return of each of these portfolios, shown in Figure 1.1.

Portfolio A in Figure 1.1 has a low expected return but low risk. Portfolio F has a high expected return but also a high level of risk. All other portfolios are somewhere between these two extremes. But notice the positions of portfolios A, B, and C. Portfolio C has the same return as A but takes more risks in getting it. Likewise, C is just as risky as B but has a lower expected return than B—that is, less bang for the risk. No rational investor would want portfolio C. Over on the high-risk end of Figure 1.1, portfolios F and G are equally risky, but F has a high expected return for the same risk.

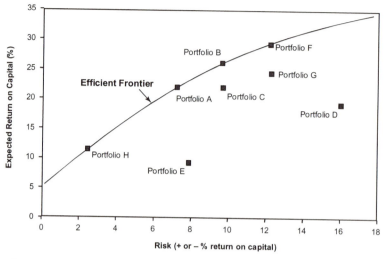

Figure 1.1 Risk-return efficient frontier.

If you were an investor-customer of the mutual-fund company, which of these portfolios would you prefer? Your choice would likely be determined by your aversion to risk or need for returns. That choice would lead you to H, A, B, or F, which give you the greatest expected return for a given level of risk. These portfolios lie along the *efficient frontier.* Portfolios C, D, E, and G have nothing to recommend them. These portfolios are inefficient.

Harry Markowitz is generally credited with formulating the theory of portfolio construction based on expected return and risk as measured by standard deviation.[8] Based on his insights and those of others in following years, financial academics developed the concept of the *efficient portfolio*—one that offers the highest expected return for a given amount of risk.

The concept of the efficient portfolio has direct applications in business management, and at many levels. The R&D manager, for example, must initiate and manage one or several portfolios, each encompassing a number of individual projects. Each project—and each portfolio—has an expected return, and the savvy manager generally has a sense of the risks inherent in each, risk being expressed as the probability of success. One of the R&D manager's jobs is to be sure that each project and each portfolio is efficient—that is, that its expected return is commensurate with the risks.

The business-unit manager is likewise responsible for creating and managing a portfolio of value-creating products and activities. So, too, is the senior corporate executive, although at a strategic level. Each of the business units under the executive's command is analogous to a security in one of the money manager's investment portfolio. Assets must be organized in ways that have the potential for creating the greatest return for a given level of risk. Risky ventures that are likely to produce no greater returns than less-risky ones must be eliminated in favor of others. When elimination is impractical or not feasible, the ventures must be reconstituted with creative alternatives to improve their risk/return characteristics. In each case, the goal is greater portfolio efficiency.

Beyond Risk and Return

The example of the investment portfolio is a useful device for understanding the concept of efficient portfolios and the efficient frontier. To the extent that business managers are obliged to view their work as a series of trade-offs between risk and return, it also has direct applications. Corporate managers, however, confront other trade-offs. Perhaps the most pressing of these is the trade-off between shareholder value and short-term earnings. On the one hand, the people who push stock prices around are keenly interested in short-term earnings. In the absence of other evidence, they use earnings as tea leaves for divining the future of the company and its market value. All protestations about the long-term view notwithstanding, investors have little patience for poor short-term earnings and the managers responsible for them.

On the other hand, the true progress of any business enterprise is measured by the long-term trajectory of its shareholder value. This is what *really* counts. Few, if any, of the activities that produced heavy-duty wealth in our lifetimes produced early short-term results. In the automotive industry, for example, the time-to-market leaders need three to four years to introduce a new car. During that period, they shell out R&D expenditures at a prodigious rate; they need at least a year of robust sales to recoup earlier investments. Prescription drugs require even longer periods to develop, test, and introduce. Most college textbooks take several years to write and one to two years to produce; even when these books are successful, many will not produce a profit for their publishers for several more years.

Everyone knows that value creation is a long-term proposition, but that knowledge has not prevented Wall Street and nervous CEOs from using short-term results as a stick with which to pound managers. Fortunately, corporations and investors are becoming more sophisticated. Shareholder value is gradually displacing short-term earnings as the metric of interest and in many companies, the basis for rewards. Several techniques have been advanced to help employees at all levels measure the extent to which their work and their decisions add or detract from shareholder value. In fact, G. Bennett Stewart and Joel Stern have built a successful consulting practice around the concept of Economic Value Added. Economic value added (EVA) has helped managers at all levels identify which of their activities create value above and beyond the firm's cost of capital and which do not. It has directed management focus away from the accounting-based measures once universally used, many of which were entirely wrongheaded.[9]

Managers can use the trade-off of short-term earnings versus shareholder value (as measured by net present value [NPV] of cash flow) to evaluate the efficiency of alternative portfolios—be they portfolios of projects or of business units. Figure 1.2 illustrates this relationship for a company. Here, the curve more closely resembles the production possibilities curve

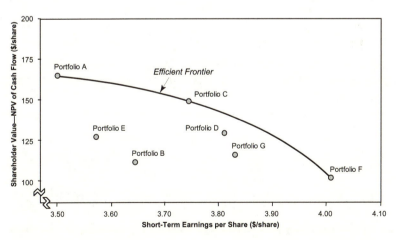

Figure 1.2 Shareholder value verses short-term earnings efficient frontier for a company.

used by economists to conceptualize trade-offs between two desirable goods (guns and butter is the classic example).

As in Figure 1.1, some portfolios in Figure 1.2 lie along the efficient frontier, while others do not. One could argue the merits of seeking portfolios A, C, and F. No case can be made, however, for seeking any of the others, as all are inefficient.

My colleagues and I regularly encounter corporations that consistently operate well below the efficient frontier. One company we worked with was far below optimal performance on virtually every efficient frontier we could concoct—risk versus returns, short-term earnings versus shareholder value, capital expenditure versus shareholder value, and so forth. This company had squandered its time and resources on a grab bag of acquisitions while overlooking a gold mine within its core businesses. The corporation's senior managers missed these opportunities because they were unable to define their efficient frontier. Once value-creating alternatives in a handful of the company's 30-plus portfolio businesses were identified, however, managers in the company were able to define their corporate efficient frontier and pursue opportunities that eventually increased share price by almost *three* times.

IDENTIFYING THE EFFICIENT FRONTIER

Our friends in the world of finance are able to identify the efficient frontier for investments, estimate the efficiency of actual portfolios, and know which money managers are doing a good job. Mountains of historical data on the individual securities and classes of securities make this possible. They know how particular stocks, for example, have behaved in the past, relative to changes in the market. They also know the total returns provided by different classes of securities (stocks, bonds, etc.) over greater or lesser periods of time. These are often good predictors of future performance. With the aid of computers, they use historical data to make inferences about the future. The business portfolio manager likewise faces the future but is less supported by historical data in making choices. Admittedly, he or she knows that if Unit A, a business operating in a mature market, just keeps on doing what it has been doing, its earnings and value creation will be more or less predictable—at least in the short run. But managers who aim for major value creation don't spend a lot of time pumping from the same wells. They focus on new opportunities whose future prospects, almost by definition, are clouded in uncertainty.

Market research and various analytical tools can help managers as they attempt to pierce the fog of uncertainty. Skillfully applied, these can help them to identify the following:

- The full range of possible outcomes.
- The impact of each of the above on earnings and share value.
- What they know, don't know, and what they need to know to make a good decision.

This is all fine in terms of making a choice about a particular project or business. Unfortunately, even a good choice—one that will result in a successful new product or put the company in a growing new market—fails to address the most important question: "Is this the *best possible* choice?" Even good choices lead to suboptimal results whenever the notion of best choices exists, which explains why even successful companies operate below the efficient frontier. Does your company's set of choices really include the *best* choices, or is it limited to the choices currently on the table?

Missing in most portfolio choices is a process for decision making that goes beyond the obvious alternatives—one that is capable of creating and objectively evaluating both existing and heretofore unimagined alternatives for value creation. The best-performing companies we encounter have this process, and they use it to pursue alternatives that define the efficient frontier. These companies reject many investment choices that their competitors would love to have!

The efficient frontier shown in Figure 1.2 identifies the best of all known portfolios for a particular company. If companies did this consistently—and well— they would greatly increase the wealth of their shareholders. They would do even better, however, if corporate and business-unit managers could work together to create even better alternatives for growth and profits—in effect, expanding the efficient frontier, as shown in Figure 1.3 for the consumer-brands company. The creation of new alternatives 1, 2, 3, and 4 in this figure has defined a new and expanded efficient frontier that has superior value.

If the conglomerate kings of decades past could be faulted for anything in particular, it was their inattention to the internal growth alternatives that could have increased shareholder wealth. The mergers that cobbled together portfolio units were often successful in raising the market multiple of the parent company's stock, but this was a one-time benefit. Financial

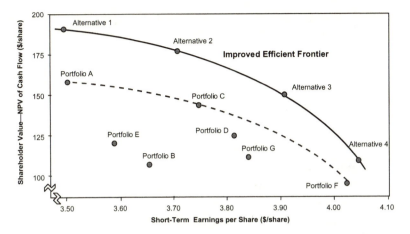

Figure 1.3 Improved efficient frontier for a consumer-brands company (shareholder value verses short-term earnings).

controls and the elimination of duplicative staff functions further boosted earnings and share values, but this, too, was a one-time fix. Lacking was a strategy and a method for fueling the growth of portfolio units. These are the dual aims of this book.

WHAT'S AHEAD

Subsequent chapters will introduce you to the concepts and methods you need to create greater value from a portfolio of individual business units—and to avoid the pitfalls of the old conglomerates. These chapters will explain the following:

- How to find the efficient frontier for your portfolio business.

- A process for developing effective portfolio strategy.
- Why real and significantly different alternatives are the key to building shareholder value—and how you can create more of them.
- Risk management in a portfolio of businesses.
- How the value contribution of each unit can be measured and tracked over time.
- The critical importance of leveraging replicable success templates—including core competencies—across the portfolio.
- How understanding business-unit life cycles can drive the search for alternatives.
- How portfolios can be strengthened through acquisition.
- How executives can use a *strategic agenda* to lead and renew the corporation and its individual units.

This book uses detailed examples throughout to illustrate these points. All are drawn from actual consulting engagements that I and my colleagues at Navigant Consulting conducted. Although the identities of the companies used in the examples have been disguised to protect proprietary information, the situations described in the book are real. The magnitude of value increases created through effective portfolio decision making are also real.

2

A Process for Portfolio Strategy Development

The failure of the conglomerates discussed in Chapter 1 was due to their inability to nurture and grow the businesses in their portfolios. A myopic focus on growth through acquisition blinded Litton Industries, ITT, and others to the need to develop internal growth opportunities for the businesses already under their umbrellas.

Despite the acquisitive orientation of their CEOs, leaders of many conglomerates and their portfolio companies *did* try to identify internal growth opportunities. Indeed, many instituted, and many still practice, annual strategic-planning exercises aimed at identifying value-creating opportunities. Unfortunately, as many know from experience, this annual exercise is often little more than a sterile, fill-in-the-blanks time waster. Every year, the forms get longer, the "Long-Term Strategic Plan" binders get thicker, and the quality of thought reaches new lows. This is unfortunate, given the importance of strategic thinking and examining current strategy.

Every business must periodically renew itself and its guiding strategy. To do otherwise is to guarantee mediocrity and eventual failure. However, strategizing on an annual basis is almost never appropriate and dissipates resources and momentum. It is like pulling a plant out of the ground to see how the roots are doing, then wondering why the plant fails to grow.

Annual corporatewide strategizing is particularly dysfunctional for portfolio companies because each operating business has its own *strategic cycle,* a period of time—measured in years—during which unit strategy must play itself out, and the strategies of different units shouldn't necessarily point in the same direction. Some business units are bound to be in an early-development stage, when new products or services are still in the pipeline and sales are small. Other portfolio businesses will be mature, harvesting fields that technology or customer tastes are gradually leaving behind; their sales are high but unlikely to grow. Still other units will be in the fast-rising middle zone between development and maturity.

Despite these very different stages, many senior executives are inclined to demand uniformity of strategy across the corporation: "We want all of our businesses to increase sales and profits by 12 percent over the next year." Unfortunately, one size does not fit all, and failing to recognize this creates wasteful misallocations of resources, as the big cash cows soak up resources in desperate but vain attempts to meet corporate growth mandates. For the corporation as a whole, those resources would produce a better outcome if they were allocated with the unique potential of each business unit in mind. Approaching businesses as though they are all the same is a sure way to destroy value.

A second reason that so many corporate planning processes fail can be found in the process itself. Think about how strategy is developed at your company. An inner circle of high-ranking executives, group managers, and staff specialists circle the wagons at some posh location and brainstorm about the future of the company. Few of the people who could contribute to this process participate; most will only hear about the company's new strategy after all the thinking has been done and all of the decisions have been made.

The term *brainstorming* is generous. In most cases, what passes for strategic thinking is little more than an exercise in which corporate managers advocate predetermined positions. Able and articulate individuals in senior positions already know where they'd like the company to be heading, and each sees his or her business unit as being a keystone in whatever plan is best for the corporation. Each pleads his or her case to the top decision makers, offering, like barrister Rumpole addressing the Bailey, whatever evidence or argument will advance the case (and keeping mum about contrary evidence). This isn't brainstorming or strategic thinking—it's selling. Information is used selectively to support a position, not to gain insight.

CEOs and their people, of course, were not born yesterday. They know how the process works and recognize that competing interests are trying to sell them on a self-interested course of action. They see their responsibility as testing each supplicant's assertions.

Their technical-staff assistants, the fact checkers, are ordered to examine the evidence and to try to identify unreasonable assumptions and implausible projections. Rivals, with plans of their own, do the same as "friends of the court." The very same process takes place at the business-unit level, as each tries to develop its contribution to the annual corporate strategy. In this courtroomlike atmosphere, the person with the best pitch or the most organizational power wins. If this process ever worked at all, it certainly doesn't work any longer, because most of the fact checkers have disappeared through waves of white-collar downsizing!

Naturally, the last thing that an advocate in this court of strategy making would do is raise either of these two important issues: alternatives and risk. Doing so would simply give ammunition to the enemy. You probably have never heard the champion of a particular project or strategy say, "Well, ladies and gentlemen, that's my plan. Of course, it's not the *only* approach we could take in reaching our goal. There are two or three others." Nor are you likely to hear this: "Now let me fill you in on the risks associated with my plan. We've estimated a 40 percent probability that our forecasted sales figure of $1.2 billion could be as low as $500 million if our competitors respond aggressively to our attempts to expand market share. In fact, $1.2 billion is our 'best case' forecast."

No, you won't hear many statements like those in decision forums that consider new projects or strategies. Whether they are driven by ambition, turfdom, or a true desire to do what's best for the corporation, advocates must sell the sizzle to gain support for their positions. The last thing they want to do is mention alternatives or point out risks. In the rare cases that these are put on the table, discussion is typically shallow. "Yes, that's an alternative, but we've already thought about it and rejected it." End of discussion. Or, "Yes, there are risks, but they aren't serious." In both cases, alternatives and risk are handled as objections to be quickly dismissed.

Eventually, someone's position carries the day, and the staff scribes set about translating the chosen strategy into its many component parts. If they do their jobs extremely well, top-level strategy will cascade downward into mid- and lower-level strategies in every business unit; each will have an aligned set of goals and budgets. Managers from top to bottom will then be drawn into seemingly endless meetings at which the specifics of goals and budgets are hammered out. Eventually, after months of work, staff people with prodigious left-brain capabilities will produce an impressive three-inch-thick binder containing a statement of corporate strategy, unit goals, and reams of budget spreadsheets. This will go into a bookcase that holds each of the previous years' versions of the same. A few pep talks will be given, employees and frontline managers—who had no input into the strategy—will yawn, and life within the corporation will return to business as usual. In most cases, the new strategy will do little to increase the value of the company.

It is easy to compare this traditional strategy process to a group of architects developing plans for a building. Working from a model of how the building should look, the architects and their assistants spend countless hours rendering blueprints that show every feature of the structure and how those features should fit together. Each wiring track and each structural interface is mapped in detail. Eventually, after months of work, the plan for the building is finished and ready to execute. However, unless someone has tested the soil and studied the load-bearing capability of the foundation, the finely crafted building may collapse. Fortunately, architects and builders give abundant attention to the foundation. Most business planners, however, do not.

THREE FOUNDATIONS OF VALUE-CREATING STRATEGY

What passes as strategic choice and planning at most corporations resembles what architects do above ground level: Executives select a strategy that has been persuasively advocated and then tell their staff people and lower-level managers to blueprint the details. After several months and thousands of man-hours, these individuals deliver an edifice of detailed plans, budgets, and spreadsheets. It's all very impressive. Unfortunately, little attention is given to the foundation upon which every strategic plan must rest:

1. Creative strategic alternatives.
2. Knowledge of how each strategic alternative will create value.
3. A clear understanding of the risks.

These are the solid cornerstones upon which strategic choice must rest. Lacking these, the most elaborately crafted strategy will quickly collapse. Unfortunately, traditional strategic decision making—the advocacy process described previously—generally ignores these foundations. Alternatives are neither sought nor systematically evaluated. The risks associated with the advocated strategy and its alternatives are neither quantified nor compared. Instead, advocates for set positions actively suppress or deflect any discussion of risk. And almost no one takes the time to measure the impact of competing strategic choices on corporate value.

Think how much more successful your corporation would be if its important choices were made from a list of practical value-creating alternatives to its current strategy, the value-creating potential of each alternative were stated, and the risks of all alternatives were clearly understood. There is little doubt that better choices would be made, your bonus would be more generous, and the shareholders' dividend checks would be bigger. Unfortunately, most companies lack an effective process and set of tools for building the foundations of good strategy at any level—at the top or within their portfolio units.

THE DIALOGUE PROCESS

The balance of this chapter describes a process and a set of analytical tools that senior executives can use to build a solid foundation for a value-creating portfolio strategy. This disciplined approach is called the *dialogue process*, because it is based on dialogue between the people responsible for making strategic decisions and allocating resources and the people responsible for implementing those decisions. This section showcases both the process and associated tools through a manufacturer of drill bits, a portfolio unit of a larger oil-field products and services corporation.

In a nutshell, the dialogue process is a multilevel, multistaged approach to collaborative decision making that does the following:

- Engages the right people and information in strategy development.
- Identifies creative and actionable alternative strategies.
- Evaluates the value and risk of each alternative.
- Selects among alternatives based on the best mix of value and risk.
- Builds the motivation and commitment for effective implementation.

There is no room in this process for unswerving advocacy, for champions, for "don't-surrender-an-inch" turf protectors, or for corporate power brokers. There are, however, many opportunities for senior executives, line managers, and technical specialists to contribute their best knowledge and insights in developing strategies that increase value. And it works.

First designed by Strategic Decisions Group (now Navigant Consulting) in 1981, the dialogue process has been used, tested, and refined through hundreds of applications in major industries—and at many levels. A recent benchmarking study (discussed further in Chapter 9) indicates that this type of process for decision making is becoming best practice in leading U.S. companies.

The process involves dialogue between two teams: (1) senior managers with the authority to make decisions and allocate resources and (2) a working group of line managers, technical specialists, and employees with unique insights into the issues—that is, the individuals closest to the opportunities of the business (see Figure 2.1). Once the decision team frames the problem and charters the process, the working group digs out the details and applies formal evaluation tools to the company's current strategy and to a realistic set of alternatives. What the process seeks, in the final analysis, are the values associated with a set of truly different practical alternatives, with full recognition of their probabilities for success or failure. The delivery of specific results at the end of each phase of this process keeps it on track and creates shared understanding and buy-in among participants.

The dialogue decision process is highly effective in doing the following:

- Exposing proposals to rational discussion.
- Requiring that alternatives be sought and evaluated.
- Creating new and superior alternatives.
- Eliminating power plays and the pursuit of personal agendas.
- Laying a solid foundation for implementation.

Figure 2.1 The dialogue process.

You'll notice six steps in the dialogue process shown in Figure 2.1:

- Step 1 produces a future-focused assessment of the business and its current strategy; it also identifies sources of value and the risks facing the business under that strategy.
- Step 2 develops creative and actionable alternative strategies that can potentially increase the value of the business.
- Step 3 evaluates each alternative strategy in terms of value and risk.
- Step 4 makes a clear choice of strategy.
- Step 5 develops the detailed implementation plan.
- Step 6 delivers the results.

Each of the first three steps is spearheaded by the working group of line and staff personnel. Dialogue with the higher-level decision team occurs at each step. This dialogue has been shown to produce higher-quality alternatives and a full understanding of the potential returns and risks facing the business. Step 4, the decision step, is where the buck stops and the resources are allocated. It is the lynchpin of the entire process. All that follows involves planning and implementation of the decision.

How does this process differ from traditional approaches to strategy development? "We do something like this," you may be saying. "We assess the current business when we do an annual plan. If it's not good enough, we come up with something else, and people are shown what they need to do to make the new strategy work." That's conventional strategy development. But ask yourself: Is your approach methodical in seeking alternatives, in weighing their potential values, and in measuring their risks? Are you maximizing the value of your corporation? Is what you do today a *process* that people can follow and improve with use, or is it an ad hoc series of meetings in which people weigh in with their views? If the answers to these questions are "no," then you do not have an effective process for delivering value—even if you are doing some of the steps in Figure 2.1.

One of the important revelations for managers over the past decade or so has been the primacy of process in doing things cheaper, faster, and better. Get the process right—and keep improving it—and great things can be accomplished. Sumantra Goshal and Christopher Bartlett have gone so far as to state that process is much more important than either organizational structure or strategy.[1] We can say no less about how strategic decisions are made. Those decisions are only as good as the process through which they are made—and only a good process can deliver a good strategy and renew it as time and changing events dictate.

The following sections consider in detail the first four steps of the dialogue decision process and the analytical tools that support it.

Step 1: Assessing the Business Situation

So much has been written on business assessment that to summarize its techniques would be less productive than focusing on what's usually missing: measurement of shareholder value and risk. Step 1 of the dialogue process aims to measure the shareholder value created by the current strategy of the business under different environmental scenarios. Every business has a current strategy. The question is: How can we measure the value and risk of this strategy? To illustrate how this is done, consider a company in the oil-field products and services business. One of its divisions manufactures drill bits. (The example is real, but the company and its division are disguised, as are all other examples in this book.) The company had a very traditional long-range planning process that updated its current strategy every year. The problem was that the drill-bit division had been mired in its current strategy for the past 10 years. The result: The drill-bit business has slipped from first to third position in the market. The corporate CEO wanted to know, "Why can't this division create more value?" To answer that question, the company needs to understand the competitive environment for this division and the different forces in that environment that will impact its strategy. An influence diagram, like the one in Figure 2.2, can help clarify which factors influence others. The influence diagram represents all major factors associated with the division and its current strategy. With the exception of the division strategy, all other factors (represented as ovals in the figure) represent uncertainties. Some are more uncertain than others.

The strategy, shown in the rectangle, includes all controllable elements: product line, R&D budget, customer-service programs, and so on. Division strategy and competitor actions clearly influence market share. Market share, market price, and market size, in turn, drive revenue. The market size of the drill-bit business is driven by oil price; drilling activity quickens as oil prices rise, and vice versa. The bottom half of Figure 2.2 shows a number of semicontrollable

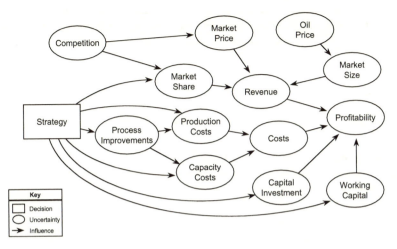

Figure 2.2 Influence diagram for the drill-bit business.

uncertainties: process-improvement success, capacity cost, the capital investment required to build new plants, and so on. The process of manufacturing rock bits is sufficiently complicated that the investment capacities and costs of new processes and plants are not entirely knowable in advance.

To measure the shareholder value and risk associated with this business, one can create a spreadsheet financial model such as the one shown in Table 2.1 (which is simplified for illustrative purposes). The model indicates that the shareholder value of the business is $767 million, as measured by the net present value of future cash flows. "Sure," you say, "if all of the assumptions are correct." The one thing that is guaranteed is that any set of assumptions over a 10-year period is not going to be correct.

In the figure, shareholder value equals the net present value (NPV) of future cash flows of the business.

Table 2.1 Drill-bit current strategy ($ and units in millions).

	Year 1		Year 4		Year 7		Year 10
Market size (units)	530	...	560	...	600	...	650
Market share (%)	14		14		14		14
Revenue ($)	222		259		311		385
Operating margin ($)	122		147		177		212
Earnings after tax ($)	75		57		82		110
Depreciation ($)	5		20		20		20
Incremental							
working capital ($)	21		3		4		5
Capital invstment ($)	12		0		1		2
Cash flow ($)	48	...	74	...	93	...	132

Shareholder value (NPV of cash flow) = $767 million.

(Net present value is the discounted sum of all future cash flows. The discount rate is the weighted average cost of capital of the corporation.)

We can utilize the spreadsheet model to identify the most important sources of business risk for our drill-bit business. Figure 2.3 shows a sensitivity analysis computed for this business. (Because of its shape, many refer to it as a *tornado chart*.) Each bar in the figure indicates the potential range of NPV that the business might eventually realize given the uncertainty inherent in each of the business variables. Thus, the actual market share captured by this business will clearly have the greatest impact on NPV. In contrast, uncertainty in capital investment or inventory turns will have minimal impact.

A quick glance at Figure 2.3 is all that is required to see where the real uncertainties that affect business value can be found. In this case, any manager who has been fixating on uncertainty in inventory turnover

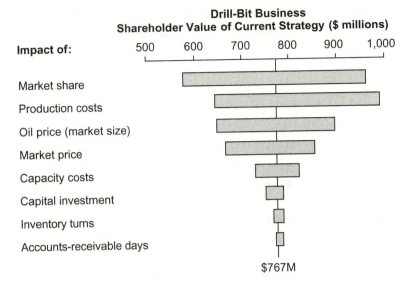

Figure 2.3 Sensitivity analysis.

could see at a glance that his or her energies and attention should instead be directed elsewhere.

The length of the bars in the tornado chart is not arbitrary but is determined through the best information, including expert judgment and research. Consider how this was done for the market-share bar in Figure 2.3. To determine the left-hand edge of the market-share bar, we went to the most knowledgeable people inside and outside the company and asked, "What market share might the company achieve, given its current strategy, such that there is only a 1 in 10 chance that market share could be lower than that number?" We then put that low-end market-share estimate into the model and determined that the value of the drill-bit business would be $575 million. On the high end, we asked a similar question: "Given its current strategy, what market-share figure could the company achieve such that there was only 1-in-10 chance that it could be higher?" Again, we put that number in the model and calculated that the value of a drill-bit business with that market share would be a little more than $960 million.

The vertical line down the middle of the tornado chart indicates the base case value of $767 million determined through the spreadsheet model. The length of the bars in the figure indicates the uncertainty associated with each risk factor. (The uncertainty [variance] is proportional to the square of the length of each bar.) In fact, the actual contribution to uncertainty is the square of the length of the bars (which is related to variance, for those who remember their statistics). Therefore, market price, which is twice the length of capacity cost, actually contributes four times as much to the uncertainty of the drill-bit business. Thus, market share, production cost, oil price, and market price contribute over 90 percent of the total uncertainty of the drill-bit business—and are the only risk factors needed in order to explore in detail for strategy!

Multiple Scenarios

In the example shown in Figure 2.3, each uncertainty varies, one at a time, while others are held at base case value. Perhaps you are thinking that "in the real world, they all vary simultaneously." And you're right. The way we deal with this is to look at multiple scenarios simultaneously.

Figure 2.4 shows a condensed version of how to generate multiple scenarios across the four critical un-

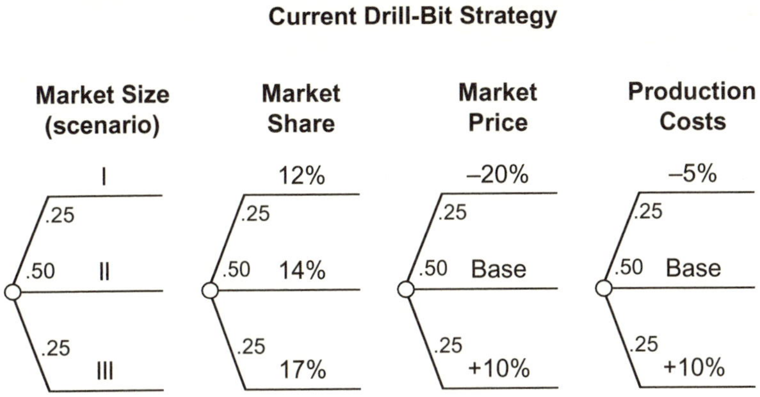

Current Drill-Bit Strategy

Market Size (scenario)	Market Share	Market Price	Production Costs

Figure 2.4 Current strategy decision tree.

certainties for the drill-bit business. Market size is shown as a scenario because it represents a combination of oil price and market size and captures both uncertainties. There are 81 possible paths through this decision tree, producing 81 unique scenarios. Each uncertainty is shown with both a value, in this example, a 12 percent market share, and a 25 percent probability that the 12 percent market-share outcome occurs. One of the 81 possible scenarios, for example, has market size scenario I, market share of 14 percent, market price of +10 percent, and production costs 5 percent below the base value. The probability of this scenario occurring is only 8 percent (multiplying $0.25 \times 0.5 \times 0.25 \times 0.25 = 7.8125$ percent, rounded up to 8 percent). Running all 81 scenarios through the spreadsheet model produces the probability distribution shown in Figure 2.5.

Figure 2.5 summarizes all scenarios for the current strategy of the drill-bit business in graphic form. The

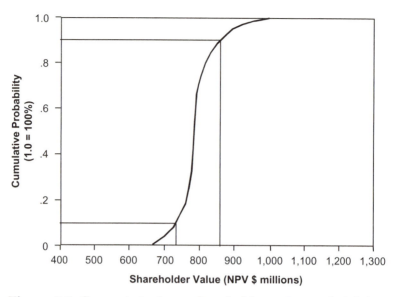

Figure 2.5 Current strategy: shareholder value and risk in the drill-bit business.

S-shaped curve measures the risk associated with that strategy. The wider the spread of the curve, the greater the risk. Because it is a *cumulative* probability curve, it reads as follows: Take any point on the curve and see where it intersects the x and y axes. For instance, in Figure 2.5, one particular point intersects the y axis at 10 percent and the x axis at roughly $730 million. This indicates that there is a 10 percent chance that the drill-bit business will be worth *less* than $730 million, given the current strategy. Choosing another point, one sees that there is also a 90 percent chance that the value of the business, given the current strategy, will be less than $860 million. The current strategy is low risk, but the drill-bit division is still stuck as number three in its industry. The CEO asks: "What are our alternatives?"

Step 2: Developing Alternative Strategies

The focus of step 2 is on developing creative alternatives to the current strategy. Because it is almost impossible for people to be simultaneously creative and analytical, companies need to suspend the analysis begun in step 1, shift gears away from the numbers, and focus on ideas.

In their book *The Smart Organization*, two of my colleagues at Navigant Consulting, Jim and David Matheson, make the point that the concept of choice is empty when there is an absence of alternatives.[2] Every organization with competent employees is capable of creating good alternatives to its current strategy. Many, however, unwittingly discourage these alternatives from coming forward by viewing people who offer them as "not on board," as "in opposition to what we're trying to accomplish," or "indecisive."

Companies that know how to create value-generating alternatives to the current strategy do not equate alternatives with opposition, disloyalty, or indecision. Instead, they foster an environment in which individual employees can objectively articulate the pros and cons of different strategies without taking sides and without a sense of advocacy. To create this type of environment, companies need to do the following:

- Suspend judgment as ideas are first proposed.
- Avoid personal criticism.
- Focus on the quantity of ideas.
- Encourage people to build on each other's ideas.
- Challenge the conventional wisdom of the business.
- Keep a record of all ideas.
- Stay alert for new ideas and allow time for their incubation.

- Avoid idea killers (e.g., "A great idea, but not for us").
- Have fun playing with different ideas.

Once many possible business ideas have been developed, take their best features and combine them into a manageable set of alternative strategies. Table 2.2 shows three alternative strategies for the drill-bit division: A, the current strategy; B, a moderate-growth strategy; and C, the Super Bits strategy. The moderate-growth strategy could make the division number two in the drill-bit industry. It entails increased R&D expenditures to expand the product line and the con-

Table 2.2 Alternative strategies for the drill-bit company.

Strategy	R&D	Manufacturing Capacity	Product Line	Staff Size
A. Current	Current R&D	Expand current plant	Current products	Current staff
B. Moderate growth	Increased R&D to expand product line, prototype shop (to cut development time by 60%)	New plant in four years	Current products, larger sizes, and evolutionary improvements	Expand staff (engineering, service, etc.) by 20%
C. Super Bits	Major R&D prototype shop, new engineers, commitment to Super Bits	New plants in four years and in nine years; Type A component manufacturing	Current products, larger sizes, and Super Bits	Expand staff (engineering, service, etc.) by 45%

struction of a new prototype shop capable of reducing product-development time by 60 percent. If this moderate-growth strategy were followed, the company would need a new manufacturing plant in approximately four years. The product line would expand and incorporate the evolutionary improvements made possible by the increased R&D expenditure and reduced development time. The company would need to increase staff size to support the increased business.

The Super Bits strategy, C, would be much different than either of the other two alternatives. It could make the division number one in its industry. Expenditures for R&D would dramatically increase, and newly hired engineers would be committed to making a revolutionary product breakthrough—a line of longer-lasting drill bits called "Super Bits." Successful development of Super Bits would double the company's market share. Two new plants would be required to meet the added demand, and employee head counts would have to expand to support the dramatic increase in business.

At this point, the division has some real alternative strategies for the drill-bit business which embody the best thinking of the business team. They offer the CEO and division management a range of choices with different resource requirements, risks, and potential outcomes. The CEO was right; there are alternatives. The question remains, "How attractive are they?"

Step 3: Evaluating the Risk and Return of the Alternative Strategies

In step 3, the dialogue shifts from discussion of potential alternatives to measuring the risk and return associated with each alternative. To do so, one utilizes the model developed in step 1 to produce a full evaluation of each alternative, with quantification of their value potentials, risks, timing, and trade-offs. Table 2.3 shows the traditional approach and results of an analysis of alternative strategies for the drill-bit business. It indicates that alternative C from Table 2.2 (Super Bits) has a shareholder value of $923 million. This is higher than either the current strategy A ($767 million) or the moderate-growth strategy B ($834 million).

But what about the uncertainties and risks associated with these strategies? Intuition cautions that the strategy with the greatest potential return may be the riskiest of the three. What is the risk that the company will fail to develop and commercialize the revolutionary new Super Bits? And what about all the other risks?

To get a better sense of the risks, let's go back to the approach used in step 1 and do a full risk analysis of all three strategies faced by the drill-bit company. The

Table 2.3 Comparison of alternative strategies for the drill-bit business.

	Year 1			Year 10		
	A	B	C	A	B	C
Market size (units)		530,000			650,000	
Market share (%)	14	14	15	14	18	25
Revenue ($M)	222	222	232	385	485	674
Variable margin ($M)	122	122	128	212	267	370
Earnings before tax ($M)	75	75	79	110	152	185
Cash Flow ($M)	48	48	48	132	165	198
Shareholder value (NPV) ($M)	767	834	923			

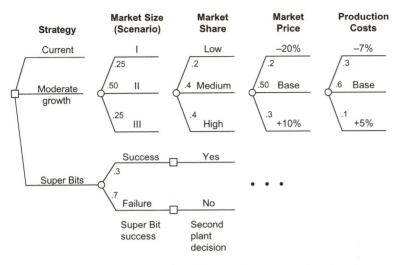

Figure 2.6 Decision tree for alternative strategies for the drill-bit business.

decision tree needed to drive the spreadsheet model is shown in Figure 2.6. Note that it now incorporates the alternative strategies and probability of success or failure of the Super Bits development project. The second plant decision is shown as contingent upon the success or failure of the Super Bit development effort. Naturally, each strategy has different market-share, market-price, production, and production-cost uncertainties. However, the model can easily deal with them.

Figure 2.7 shows the cumulative probability distribution on shareholder value for the three alternative strategies based on the decision tree. One can see at a glance that the moderate-growth and Super Bits alternatives are substantially more risky but also potentially more rewarding in terms of shareholder values than the current strategy. The expected value of the

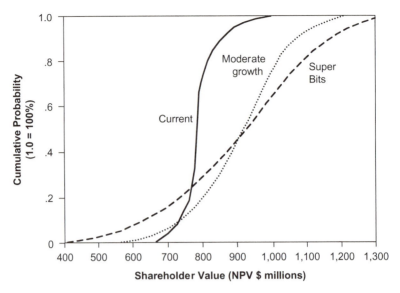

Figure 2.7 Risk and return of alternative strategies for the drill-bit business.

moderate-growth and Super Bits strategies are nearly the same. (The expected value is the probability weighted value, calculated by the sum of the NPV of each scenario times its probability.) However, the Super Bits strategy contains much more risk, including upside potential as well as downside. The upside areas on the graph for Super Bits correlate with Super Bits' development success, and the downside areas correlate with the failure of the product team to produce a truly revolutionary product.

Most managers would select the moderate-growth strategy because of its overall risk and return characteristics. They can see that it has far greater upside potential than the current strategy, with very little chance of producing an inferior result. The Super Bits strategy, in comparison, offers the highest potential NPV outcome but not *much* more upside than the moderate-growth strategy. At the same time, there is a large chance that its actual NPV will be less than the moderate-growth or the current strategy. In fact, this Super Bits strategy presents a wide spectrum of potential outcomes (more risk) when compared to the other two alternatives. By recasting the data in the same kinds of bars used in Figure 2.3, the tornado chart, the probability distribution of each alternative become more apparent (see Figure 2.8).

As in Figure 2.3, the high-value end of each bar in Figure 2.8 represents the shareholder value such that there is only a 10 percent chance of the value being greater than the number shown, and the low-value end represents shareholder value such that there is only a 10 percent chance of shareholder value being less than the value shown. The line in the middle is the expected value of the strategy. Figure 2.8 shows

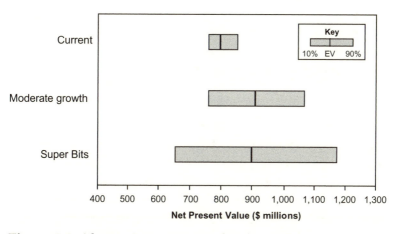

Figure 2.8 Alternative strategies for the drill-bit business, 10 to 90 percent ranges.

that the moderate-growth strategy adds $110 million to the expected value of the division with little risk. The Super Bits strategy can add almost as much, but at the cost of substantial added risk to the division.

Step 4: Deciding among the Alternatives

The objective in step 4 is to select the best possible strategy from a manageable set of objectively evaluated alternatives. Because of the work done up to this point, the decision team is in a good position to do this. The data represented in Figures 2.7 and 2.8 reflect the best estimates by the best-informed people about the risks and returns associated with the current strategy and two very good alternatives. The decision makers can then ask the hard questions:

> "Do we have the resources and the commitment to successfully implement any of these alternatives?"
> "Is the corporation in a position to bear the risks associated with these alternatives?"
> "Should we make a decision now or try to reduce some of the uncertainties associated with these choices first?"

Because decisions involve the future, no amount of work by participants in the dialogue process can produce a perfect no-brainer choice for the decision team. However, the example of the drill-bit company should make it clear that this process can improve the odds that strategic decisions will result in greater value creation for the organization. It may be less than perfect, but it is far superior to the process of advocacy through which most decisions are currently made.

Once the leadership makes a decision, they must commit the resources required to implement it and assign appropriate responsibility for implementation. If drill bits were the only division of the corporation, this would be simple. However, the drill-bit division is but one of many oil-field and engineering businesses in this corporate portfolio. The corporation cannot allocate its resources in isolation; it must look across the entire portfolio to allocate its resources to its best opportunities. This is exactly what so many portfolio companies fail to do. In effect, they try to make everything grow in equal measure—and it simply doesn't work.

Once the selection of the best strategic alternative is made, the decision team and working groups of staff and line managers can move on to the development of budgets and action plans in step 5, and then implementation in step 6. The methods of steps 5 and 6 are outside the scope of this book but are familiar to many readers.

DIALOGUE LEADS TO BETTER STRATEGY

The decision process just described aims to identify and channel resources to the strategic alternatives with the best risk-return characteristics. The tone of this process is one of objectivity, open-mindedness, and discovery. Decisions are not tipped in the direction of the best connected, the deal makers, or the shrillest voices. Unlike the highly politicized advocacy process it replaces, the outcome of the dialogue process cannot be known in advance. Surprise is one of its great benefits.

The dialogue process is broad based and engages the right people—executives with the authority to allocate resources and make decisions stick, staff specialists with the numbers, and line managers and sales people who have their thumbs on the pulse of the business and its competitive environment. Collectively, these are the same people who must be sold on the virtues of any new strategy and then carry it forward.

How does this strategic decision process compare with the one your organization uses?

3

The Efficient Frontier

Chapter 1 defined the efficient frontier as the best set of trade-offs between risk and long-term wealth creation, or between short-term earnings and long-term wealth creation. Major corporations regularly operate well inside their own efficient frontiers. In many cases, senior managers miss opportunities simply because they cannot visualize the efficient frontier that defines the important trade-off between building shareholder value and short-term earnings. This chapter will show you how you can use the dialogue process described in Chapter 2 to define the efficient value frontier for your organization. Once that frontier is defined, you will be in a position to determine which set of business unit and unit strategies, that is, which portfolio, represents the highest value-creating potential for the corporation as a whole. You will also be able to recognize what it takes to get it.

FROM BUSINESS UNIT
TO CORPORATE PORTFOLIO STRATEGY

Thus far, this book has concentrated on business-unit decisions, using the dialogue process to assess the current business and surface alternatives and to evaluate each alternative. The goal has been to optimize the set of activities pursued by the business unit in terms of risk and returns, or other sets of trade-offs. The dialogue process is equally effective for strategy making at the portfolio level. Instead of focusing interest and analysis on individual business-unit activities, however, the dialogue process considers the risks and potential returns of different *portfolios*. Thinking and analysis moves up a notch in the hierarchy of corporate decisions (Figure 3.1) to portfolio strategy and the selection of business-unit strategies.

Portfolio strategy is at the heart of a multibusiness company because decisions made at that level determine how corporate resources can be best allocated. Resource allocation could simply be an exercise in taking away resources from the units that have performed least well and directing them to the units that have performed best in the most recent period. Indeed, that is exactly what many corporate pension-fund managers do each year when they farm out the billions in the pension fund to the different money managers they employ. Looking back over the previous two or three years, and using a risk-adjusted index of returns, they find, for example, that Wall Street Pension Wunderkinds has had two lousy years, but

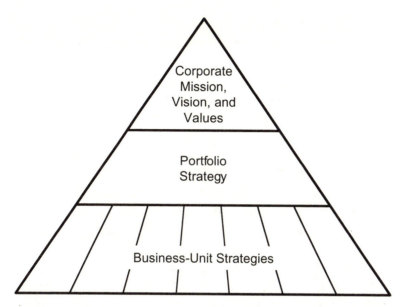

Figure 3.1 Corporate portfolio decision hierarchy.

Fleet Street Fund Gurus has done exceptionally well. "So, for the coming year," the manager decides, "we'll move some of our chips from Wall Street's pile over to Fleet Street's. It's always best to ride the winning ponies." This would be a good way to allocate pension money if the future performance of the two fund managers in question could be expected to be a repeat of the past.

Likewise, the different units of a multibusiness corporation represent the corporation's overall portfolio. Allocating resources to value-producing strategies among these units allows the enterprise to grow in the direction of the greatest opportunity. A corporation's resources need to be allocated to those units with the greatest potential for building future value. Doing so simply on the basis of past performance, however, could be fatal.

Portfolio decisions can eventually shape corporate strategy at the top (mission, vision, and values) because following the trail of growth can influence the direction of a company as a whole. Portfolio strategy opportunities also often strongly influence and sometimes drive corporate financial strategy. Indeed, it is not unusual for a major corporation to undergo a metamorphosis driven by the various successes and opportunities of its portfolio units. These enterprises follow the trail of opportunity like hounds on a scent. As the hunt takes them into new territory, they change though a process of adaptation, gaining new competencies, new market understandings, and capabilities to fit the need and bringing in new people.

Hewlett-Packard is a good example of this type of portfolio strategy. The company's origin is in the electronic test-and-measurement equipment business, but its different units—spawned by invention or observed opportunity—have remade the image of the corporation over the years. The pursuit of opportunity in high-end calculators, computer workstations, laser and ink-jet printers, and more recently, personal computers has, over time, enormously reshaped this company. In effect, these portfolio units have largely defined what people think of as the Hewlett-Packard corporation. Hewlett-Packard is spinning off its instrument business in response to changing markets and business opportunities. These changes demonstrate how portfolio management can change the face of the corporation as a whole.

Bartlett and Ghoshal have noted that good management processes disseminate organizational learning both horizontally and vertically.[1] Good portfolio management process—based on dialogue—does the same.

Dialogue and the objective discussion of risk builds a culture of trust.

Unfortunately, a portfolio strategy that simply moves resources away from lagging units toward growing ones, although intuitively appealing, will not assure the outcome that executives bargained for because a few important pieces are missing:

1. *It is backward looking.* Exceptional past performance should be rewarded, but decision making aims for the future. Portfolio strategists must know and understand the opportunities.

2. *There is no clear link between risk and return for future ventures.* The investment management business has a number of measures for adjusting past returns with the risks taken to get them. One can objectively rate the past performance of money managers on a risk-adjusted basis. Chapter 2 describes one approach to measuring risk for business-unit projects. But to date, few corporations are aware of it. Companies that cannot communicate about risk cannot build environments of trust in which necessary risks will be taken to superior returns.

3. *It overlooks opportunities that exist within its own units.* One of the big failings of the conglomerate CEOs was an impatience with the basics of business development. Quality-based improvements, R&D, joint ventures aimed at breaking through market barriers, and so forth didn't interest them. They were too impatient and too accustomed to creating paper profits through the buying and selling of companies. The slow but steady stewardship that builds value from new ideas, customer relationships, and organizational development was not their style. The portfolio strate-

gist who behaves like the corporate pension manager isn't much different. Although mergers and acquisitions have an important place in value creation, they are no substitute for building value internally.

TOWARD THE EFFICIENT FRONTIER

Every multiunit corporation is a portfolio of current and potential opportunities. Your own corporation, for example, probably has several divisions, subsidiaries, or profit centers and a number of ideas for expanding, contracting, or refocusing these units—some good, some not so good. If managers were actively encouraged to seek alternatives, as advised in Chapter 2, this set of opportunities could be expanded manyfold.

If you took the time and trouble to evaluate these opportunities and plot them in terms of risk versus potential reward, or NPV versus short-term earnings, or NPV versus capital expenditures, you would see that some would be optimal while others would be suboptimal. Let's see how this works with a real but disguised pharmaceutical company called "Mega-Pharma."

MegaPharma is currently in five main businesses:

1. Worldwide pharmaceuticals.
2. Consumer products.
3. Fine chemicals.
4. Specialty chemicals.
5. Agricultural products.

Using a dialogue process such as the one described in Chapter 2, a corporate-level team of decision makers and working teams of corporate staff and unit managers go through the process of evaluating the current strategy of the corporation, as well as a set of alternative opportunities that exist within each of its five operating units. (It also considers several possible financial strategies). For example, the worldwide pharmaceuticals unit has developed five alternative strategies for growing its business:

- Short-term profit improvement and risk reduction.
- Current broad-based strategy.
- Focused reallocation.
- Joint venture and license focused.
- Broad expansion.

The teams have carefully evaluated each of these strategies in terms of likely ranges of NPV. In other words, they have explored each strategy in terms of the analysis demonstrated in Chapter 2. This level of specificity is essential in order to measure the shareholder value and risk associated with each strategy.

Table 3.1, a *strategy table*, lists, in the vertical columns, the set of alternatives identified and evaluated for each operating unit. Cutting laterally across the columns indicated in boxes is just one of thousands of possible routes MegaPharma executives could take in constructing a portfolio strategy for their five-unit company. In this example the overriding strategy was to refocus on key opportunities. Selecting one alternative from each column in the table, this strategy aims for focused reallocation in its worldwide pharmaceutical unit, focuses on over-the-counter for its consumer-products units, sells the specialty chemicals unit, and so forth. Together, these alternatives

Table 3.1 Constructing a portfolio strategy.

Strategy	Worldwide Pharmaceuticals	Consumer Products	Fine Chemicals	Specialty Chemicals	Agricultural Products	Financial Policy
A. Current	Short-term profit improvement and risk reduction	Beauty products focus	Support current and new pharmaceutical products	Continue as is with limited investment	Sell	Continue to increase dividends
B. Improve current earnings	Current broad-based strategy	Beauty and skin care focus		New product focus to increase market share	Support current products and product development	Raise debt rating, lower dividends
C. Focus on pharmaceuticals	**Focused reallocation**	Sell beauty products and retrench to OTC (over-the-counter) proprietaries	**Invest to become low-cost producer of key generics**	**Sell**	**Expand into herbicides**	**Constant dividends**
D. Refocus on key opportunities	Joint venture and license focus	**Focus on OTC and expand with prescription drug to OTC program**	Support all products			
E. Aggressive expansion	Broad-based expansion				Broad animal health and herbicide products	

represent a particular portfolio strategy for Mega-Pharma.

There are over 2,100 potential portfolio strategies in this strategy table. If each of these was thoroughly evaluated in terms of NPV and potential short-term earnings, they could be plotted in a scattergram such as shown in Figure 3.2. The few that lie along or very near the line of the efficient frontier optimize the two desired values: NPV and short-term earnings. If MegaPharma executives were intent on maximizing expected NPV, for instance, they would be attracted to strategy E, aggressive expansion. On the other hand, if short-term earnings were their commanding interest, portfolio strategy B, improving current earnings, would maximize their intent. Other portfolio strategies lying on or very near the frontier would allow

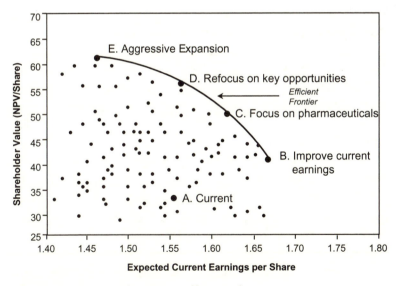

Figure 3.2 MegaPharma's efficient frontier.

them to balance these two goals—giving up some NPV to gain more short-term earnings, and vice versa.

What must be avoided, of course, are the many portfolio strategies that lie below the efficient frontier—A, the current strategy, being a perfect example. This strategy delivers a fairly high level of short-term earnings, which may be just what decision makers want. However, plenty of alternatives in the scattergram deliver the same level of short-term earnings as well as a higher NPV. Portfolio strategy D is the best of these. As long as D is a viable option, no rational decision maker would ever consider the current strategy. Unfortunately, many corporations, without knowing it, do just that, and the reason is simple: They have not been able to quantify the value of their current strategies or their alternatives. In most cases, they don't know what the alternatives are. Unless it takes the time and trouble to identify alternatives and evaluate them quantitatively, a company cannot know where it stands relative to the universe of possible portfolio strategies. The efficient frontier is then nothing but a theoretical concept.

Of course, evaluating 2,000 or more possibilities would cause brain-cell meltdown in the working team charged with doing the number crunching. Fortunately, managers and analysts in tune with the dynamics of the different businesses can usually identify a manageable number of alternative strategies with the greatest potential and weed out the weaklings. In addition, each portfolio strategy on the efficient frontier takes the corporation in a new direction, with different mixes of business units, resources, and core competencies. It would be nice if one could simply find the best alternative in each column of the strategy table and string them together as a portfolio. Unfortunately, this is not effective because what is best for a particular business unit is rarely best for the corporation as a whole. Yet, this is what most planning processes deliver to the CEO.

Once the strategies are plotted, interpretation is straightforward. For example, simply eyeballing the values on the two axes for portfolio E indicates that this portfolio strategy gives MegaPharma an opportunity to nearly double its shareholder value over its current strategy. The cost of following this strategy is about 6 percent of current short-term earnings. (Although the numbers for this particular corporation are disguised, these figures are typical of what I see in consulting assignments.)

MegaPharma, like virtually all of the clients that my colleagues and I have seen in well over 100 consulting engagements, is operating well inside its efficient frontier, maximizing neither short-term earnings nor long-term shareholder value. The common reason for this is that these companies have not developed creative and actionable alternatives focused on increasing shareholder value; nor have they built the analytical infrastructure needed to evaluate the shareholder value and risk of the corporation and its operating units. Chapter 4 explores the problem of not developing attractive alternatives.

EXPANDING THE FRONTIER

Executives of MegaPharma were highly pleased with the new portfolio opportunities available to them; all were better than the current strategy and provided a real choice of corporate direction. However, the executives should never view this opportunity set as a closed book. The set of possible alternatives is bound only by the imagination of employees and managers and can be expanded through the development of new alternatives and through possible acquisitions. Figure 3.3 shows how the development of new and better alternatives can expand the frontier of value and opportunity.

The enterprises that are admired for their growth and vitality continually expand the frontier of their value-creating opportunities. For example, ink-jet printer technology developed by Hewlett-Packard engineers expanded the company's efficient frontier by opening up a large new set of opportunities and a multibillion-dollar printer business. Xerox's amazing laboratory successes with laser printing and personal computing technology accomplished the same, but for rivals Apple and Microsoft![2]

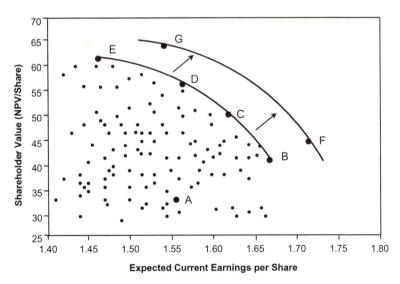

Figure 3.3 The efficient frontier expanded.

Merger and acquisition opportunities, which are constantly being presented to corporate management, have the potential to expand the frontier. Of course, the ill-advised sale or acquisition of portfolio units can do just the opposite. Business history is full of examples of acquisition deals that lay well *inside* the existing efficient frontier. Indeed, a great deal of time and treasure has been wasted over the years on corporate restructurings that, when the dust settled, left companies poorer for the experience (this is discussed further in Chapter 8). One dramatic example is AT&T's 1991 acquisition of National Cash Register (NCR). Ostensibly acquired to provide AT&T with a beachhead in computing and to promote growth, NCR passed through AT&T like a stone, destroying billions of dollars of value in the process. Ironically, this occurred at a time when AT&T was losing long-distance market share to more nimble competitors and the telecommunications industry, of which it was the de facto leader, was awash in value-creating opportunities, including local access, wireless telephony, and the Internet, among many others. The opportunities were there, but AT&T seemed to lack a mechanism capable of finding and developing them.

WHAT ABOUT RISK?

At this point, you are probably thinking, "What about the risks associated with each of the points on the efficient frontier? Could the choice of one of these launch MegaPharma onto a risky course it doesn't understand?" This is an important question because no strategic choice should ever be made before its risks are diligently explored. Every executive understands this, but in the absence of quantitative methods to assist them, most follow a seat-of-the-pants approach to risk assessment. This is better than nothing, but often not much better.

The classic efficient frontier is cast against the dimensions of risk and return, making risk obvious. But what if one chooses to evaluate portfolio strategies in terms of return and some other measure, such as short-term earnings? Does this eliminate the possibility of assessing risk? Fortunately, it does not. You simply must do some additional work—namely, determine a range of probabilities associated with each strategy. Chapter 2 demonstrated a method for doing this, developing measures of risk and return for a number of alternatives for a single business unit. The same can be done, for the different portfolio strategies available to MegaPharma, as shown in Figure 3.4.

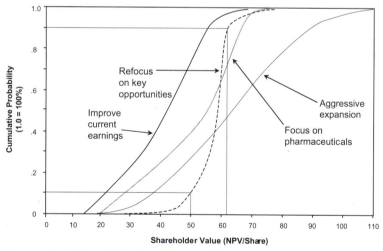

Figure 3.4 The risk of each portfolio strategy.

Figure 3.4 indicates the probability that the share-holder value of the corporation with the portfolio strategy in place will be less than or equal to a particular shareholder value on the bottom axis. The spread of the curve for each strategy indicates the magnitude of the risk. The refocus strategy involves less risk than the other strategies. For example, there is approximately an 80 percent probability that the refocus on key opportunities strategy will produce NPV between $50 and $62 per share. By comparison, the NPV produced by the aggressive expansion strategy is potentially all over the map—the chance of it producing less than $36 per share is about the same as the chance that it will ring the cash register at more than $88 per share. MegaPharma would run a much lower risk if it adopted the refocus strategy. However, the higher potential payoff of the aggressive-expansion strategy could prompt MegaPharma executives to opt for it, even though it has much higher risk than the refocus strategy.

The focus-on-pharmaceuticals strategy actually has a large chance of being worse than the refocus-on-key-opportunities strategy. It is important to note that the focus-on-pharmaceuticals strategy is not a pure-play strategy and that no pure-play strategies emerged on the efficient frontier for this corporation. To understand why, one needs to recognize that all of Mega-Pharma's business units are adding shareholder value. Although it is possible to create more share-holder value by divesting certain units and plowing the cash back into others (for example, sale of the specialty-chemicals unit), no single business unit maximizes shareholder value given the actionable alternative strategies that MegaPharma has been able to create.

Defining the Efficient Frontier

The MegaPharma case provides an overview of how the dialogue process can be used to determine a company's efficient frontier. The following discussion explores the details for an expense-intensive company.

Consider the example of a consumer packaged-goods company whose brands are all household names, "CPG, Inc." It is a matrix organization in which the geographic businesses are the business units and its categories of consumer products are managed by worldwide category executives. To simplify the discussion, which is based on a disguised version of a real company, the example will focus on only four categories of products (personal hygiene, cosmetics, oral care, and household cleaning) and three geographic areas: North America, Europe (including Eastern Europe), and international (the rest of the world). The key question confronting CPG management is how to create more shareholder value.

Assessing the Current Portfolio Strategy

The first thing CPG managers need to do is assess the current portfolio strategy and its value. In this case, there was already strategy in the company's set of business plans and five-year business projections. This strategy embodies a number of business actions. For example, the current strategy of the personal-hygiene category includes a number of challenging initiatives:

- Continued introduction of existing brands into China and Eastern Europe.

- Development and launch of an extra-strength product to serve the premium-market segment.
- Development and introduction of a children's product.
- Numerous line extensions and continuing product enhancements.

The current strategy for the cosmetics category includes the following:

- Brand line extensions.
- Worldwide launch of a new brand.
- Line extensions for three high-potential, regional brands.

To evaluate the contribution to shareholder value of each of the four product categories, the company needs to create a shareholder value model such as the one described in Chapter 2. Figure 3.5 utilizes the shareholder-value model to show the value and risk profile of the current strategy for each category.

Risk factors include the following:

- Product performance and technical uncertainties associated with developing specific new products.
- Competitor actions that influence market share or price levels.
- Future premiums commanded by highly supported brands versus generic or unsupported brands.
- Customer response to perceived product differences and positioning of products.
- Tariff and local manufacturing requirements.
- Advertising strategy effectiveness.

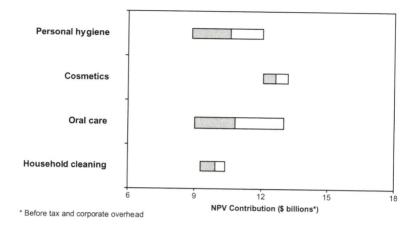

Figure 3.5 Risks and returns of CPG's current category strategies (NPV contributions in $ billions).

There is a 10 percent probability that the NPV contribution will be less than the left-hand edge of each bar and a 10 percent chance that the contribution will be higher than the right-hand edge. The line in the middle indicates the expected value. The width of each bar, then, represents the range of possible outcomes representing an 80 percent probability interval and is determined by the risks associated with each category of business. The greater the risks associated with a product category, the wider the bar. For example, the base case for the cosmetics business appears to be worth approximately $12.6 billion; the narrow range of likely outcomes (from $12 billion to $13.2 billion) indicates a low level of risk. The oral product line, in contrast, contains a much higher level of uncertainty.

Beyond the Current Strategies

Using the analysis illustrated in Figure 3.5, corporate executives can see at a glance the range of likely shareholder values for each product category, given their current strategies. The length of the value bars differentiates the risky and not-so-risky ventures.

But why should one assume that CPG's current strategies are best? Isn't it possible—indeed, *likely*—that each of its product categories contains more potential value than are represented in the current case? Jim and David Matheson have articulated what many managers know subconsciously: Big corporations unknowingly and routinely encourage a culture of suboptimization. The best strategies are not always brought to the table. Why not? You can probably answer this question as well as anyone: Because suggesting something different might step on the toes of some politically dangerous executive; because doing so may be personally too risky; because it's better to be safe than sorry. The Mathesons have this to say:

> The manager who develops a project plan with a 55 percent chance of adding $1 million to next year's revenues finds that the boss has turned the $1 million into a *goal* and created a 45 percent chance that he will not make his bonus. . . . Companies also have a bad habit of shifting the risk of failure from the larger organization (which can bear risk through diversification) to individual employees (who cannot). This creates situations in which employees will pursue a low-risk strategy . . . and ignore a higher risk strategy whose range of possible returns is *at least* as high as the low-risk alternative.[3]

Does this sound familiar?

One of CPG's key goals in using the dialogue process was to actively encourage business-unit managers and personnel to think outside the lines of current strategies and seek out alternatives with greater potential value. Each category team was, in fact, asked to develop an aggressive-growth strategy—one that would describe what the business might look like in 10 years if resources were not constrained. They then fleshed out these visions with the major activities needed to realize them over the next five years, together with a rough assessment of the risks and potential rewards.

Figure 3.6 shows the result of CPG's work. As illustrated in the figure, each product category's potential new strategy has greater value than its current strategy. As to be expected, some of these are also riskier than the current strategy.

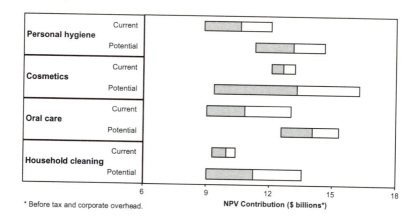

Figure 3.6 Potential risks and returns of categories.

For example, a $1 billion expected (the center line) increase in the value of the cosmetics business over the current strategy goes hand-in-hand with a nearly six-fold increase in uncertainty. This greater risk, as the category team explained, is associated with the world-wide launch of a new brand and other initiatives. If these initiatives are successful, they conclude, the po-tential shareholder value of the cosmetics business will be above $17 billion. However, there is a 90 percent chance that the outcome will be less than $17 billion, and a 1-in-10 chance that it will be as low as $9.5 bil-lion—far below the worst case of the current strategy.

Figure 3.7 shows an efficient frontier that incor-porates the current strategies of the portfolio of consumer-brands businesses versus the potential identified within the portfolio. It indicates a potential to increase shareholder value by more than 40 percent at the cost of roughly 13 percent in average earnings per share for the next three years.

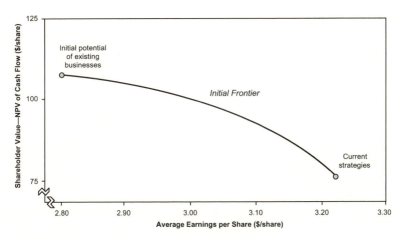

Figure 3.7 Initial CPG efficient frontier.

Developing Portfolio Alternatives

Chapter 2 showed a graphic representation of the dialogue process (Figure 2.1) that businesses can use to create greater value, describing each step in terms of the individual business unit. The present chapter has been following this same process in discussing CPG. The only difference is that everything has moved up from the business unit to the corporate portfolio level, as shown in Figure 3.8. The strategy teams are now corporate executives and key staff people on the top line and business-unit people on the bottom line. These individuals comprise the two teams between which dialogue and decision making occur.

At this point, the company has already been through step 1 of the dialogue process—assessing the current business. Furthermore, "what-if" questions within each of CPG's product groups have determined that much more could be gained by the corpo-

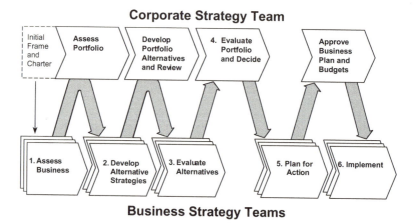

Figure 3.8 The corporate-level dialogue process.

ration if these units were more aggressive in pursuing new strategies. But so far, no one has systematically developed or reviewed alternative strategies for the product categories. That is the task of step 2 of the process—to identify the most attractive business initiatives and formulate alternative strategies that include the business initiatives, any acquisition opportunities, and other attractive initiatives not yet considered. This step can also be utilized to understand any corporate value trade-offs (such as risk versus return). Finally, the company can use this step to fill information gaps: potential competitor responses to CPG's initiatives, political or regulatory uncertainties, R&D risks, and the potential value of continuous-improvement programs.

The teams at CPG managed to develop four alternatives to the current strategy:

1. *Improved plan.* Enhance the current strategy with high return initiatives that have a one- to three-year payback.
2. *Key opportunities.* Complement improved-plan investments with product enhancements and geographic expansion for high-potential brands.
3. *Aggressive growth.* Invest in key brands that have very productive opportunities for long-term growth.
4. *All opportunities.* Invest in every major opportunity that has a positive expected NPV.

They then took the time to do the detailed analytical work needed to estimate the contribution NPV (i.e., NPV before overhead, tax, and interest) of each of the four new alternative strategies. Table 3.2 shows those values and their sources for just one of the product

Table 3.2 Alternatives for the personal-hygiene product category.

Category Initiative	Improved Plan	NPV of Contribution	Key Opportunities	NPV of Contribution	Aggressive	NPV of Contribution	All Opportunities	NPV of Contribution
China	0		X	2100	X	2100	X	2100
India	0		Partial	440	Partial	440	X	465
Latin America	0		0		0		X	390
Increased Advertising	X	1100	X	1100	X	1100	X	1100
Eastern Europe	0		0		0		X	315
Indonesia	0		0		X	120	X	120
Extra-strength/premium brand (Europe)	0		0		0		X	155
Extra-strength/premium brand (International)	0		0		0		X	360
Base-brand relaunch	0		X	875	X	875	X	875
New brand (North America)	0		X	410	X	410	X	410

categories—personal hygiene. An x in the first column for each alternative strategy indicates that the initiative is included in the strategy. The second column of each strategy shows the NPV contribution (in $ millions) of each initiative.

In this particular example, shareholder value is increased primarily by globalization of existing products, product advertising, and the development of new products. However, the CPG working team considered many other types of value-enhancing initiatives, including manufacturing and productivity improvements, as well as the acquisition of brands in specific countries. Obviously, the contribution of these initiatives had to incorporate their probabilities of success. For example, contribution NPV's from manufacturing improvements had to consider the probability of successfully developing new process equipment capable of reducing manufacturing costs.

Detailed analysis by the CPG working team extended to all of the important particulars of the four new alternative strategies. For example, Table 3.3 indicates that the alternatives have substantially different incremental launch costs above the current planned strategy and that the emphasis of product launches varies substantially between the alternative strategies.

By this point, the CPG team had defined alternative portfolio strategies (improved plan, key opportunities, aggressive, and all opportunities) in a way that ensured that all were on or near the efficient frontier. They constructed these alternatives to pick the highest "bang-for-the-buck" initiatives first from those available for each category. Table 3.2 shows this for the personal-hygiene product category. Chapter 7 discusses how to calculate bang for the buck.

Table 3.3 CPG portfolio-resource alternatives. Incremental cost of alternatives* ($ millions/year).

	Improved Plan	Key Opportunities	Aggressive	All Opportunities
Increased base business advertising	42	57	63	102
Launching existing products in new geographies	12	60	126	225
Launching new products	6	111	153	222
Total	60	228	342	549

*Average from 1996 to 2001.

Evaluate and Decide

Steps 3 and 4 of the dialogue process call for evaluation of alternative portfolio strategies and a decision by the corporate team. The goal of evaluating the portfolio alternatives is to clearly understand the implications of choosing one portfolio strategy over another. To do this, the evaluation must deliver the following results:

1. Optimized alternatives that lie on the efficient frontier.
2. Fully evaluated alternatives with quantification of the following:
   - Shareholder value.
   - Annual shareholder value added.
   - Earnings.
   - Risks.
   - Timing.

3. Clearly define the trade-offs associated with selecting one alternative over the other.

Figure 3.9 shows the efficient frontier for CPG's portfolio alternatives. Again, it preserves the relative magnitudes of average earnings per share and shareholder value that were observed in the actual CPG case. Both the initial potential of existing business and the current strategy, like so many companies observed in practice, are beneath the efficient frontier, indicating the level to which CPG is currently suboptimizing shareholder value and current earnings.

CPG's current portfolio strategy, however, was as near to the efficient frontier as my colleagues and I have ever observed. It was truly a well-run company! However, its all-opportunities alternative had the potential to increase shareholder value by as much as 60 percent at the cost of a 20 percent impact on earnings per share or less. The improved-plan strategy would potentially increase shareholder value *and* average

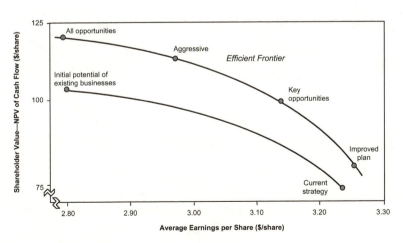

Figure 3.9 CPG portfolio alternatives.

earnings relative to the current strategy. And the key-opportunities strategy indicated a shareholder value increase of 30 percent at the cost of 3 percent of current earnings. Note that the initial frontier is well inside of the efficient frontier formed by these superior alternatives.

This illustrates the true worth of dialogue process. By going through the process, CPG learned how to increase value substantially, as well as the mechanisms for doing so. The company refocused its efforts on the aggressive strategies it selected. Equally important, it continued to use the process to improve its efficient frontier.

Figure 3.10 shows the after-tax profit alternatives associated with the efficient frontier. Note that even the improved plan required some decrease in 1996 earnings even though it produced improved earnings overall in the first three years (1996, 1997, and 1998). The all-opportunities alternative that creates the most shareholder value does not catch up with the current

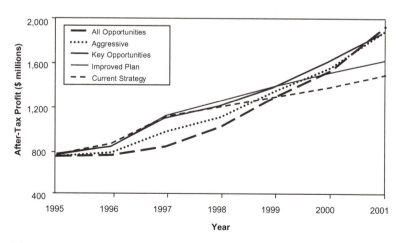

Figure 3.10 CPG portfolio after-tax profits.

strategy until year four (1999). Figure 3.10 illustrates the dilemma one faces in picking one point instead of another on the efficient frontier. Nevertheless, well-run companies with good reputations can make the case to stakeholders for investing earnings long-term to build shareholder value. For example, one pharmaceutical client recently succeeded in strengthening its product pipeline as a result of increasing its development expenditures by 50 percent. Investors responded by bidding up the company's stock despite the negative impact of those increased expenditures on current earnings.

But what about the risks? Figure 3.11 shows the risks associated with each alternative strategy: The risks increase as the strategies become more aggres-

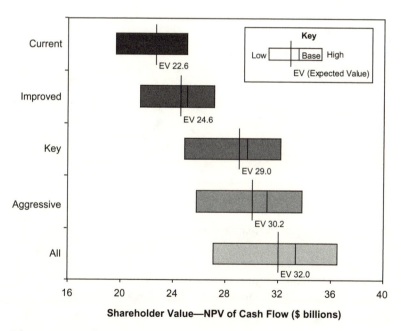

Figure 3.11 Consumer brands portfolio risks.

sive. As seen with MegaPharma, however, this is not always the case. It is true for this example because the overriding risk factors are associated with global uncertainties such as brand-pricing differentials, regulation, risk factors of new markets such as China and Eastern Europe, and global trade.

The risk analysis shown in Figure 3.11 provides considerable insight into the risks that CPG is undertaking. As its strategies become more aggressive, there is more risk associated with each one (the bars get longer). One can also see from Figure 3.11 that the base cases are more optimistic than the expected values. This is often the case and is one of the reasons that a careful risk analysis is so valuable.

Some managers can better appreciate the risk-return relationship if the information is given via the graph form traditionally used by investors, as in Figure 3.12,

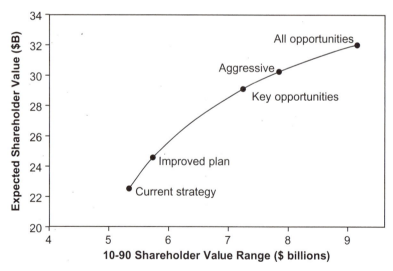

Figure 3.12 Risk efficient frontier.

which shows CPG's *risk efficient* frontier. As with all efficient frontiers, the left-hand axis is shareholder value (in this case *expected* shareholder value). The bottom axis is determined by the length of the bars shown in Figure 3.11 (the 10 to 90 shareholder range). Remember, the greater the length, the greater the uncertainty associated with each strategy. There is a 10 percent chance that the actual value will be less than the left edge of each bar, and a 10 percent chance that the actual value will be greater than the right edge of each bar. Thus, 80 percent of the outcomes will fall inside each bar—a 10 to 90 percent range.

The risk efficient frontier clearly indicates the trade-offs between building shareholder value and the risks incurred in pursuing them. Together with the short-term-earnings frontier shown in Figure 3.9, it provides senior management with an understanding of the trade-offs needed to select CPG's portfolio strategy.

Risk versus return is not the only trade-off managers must consider. Others include short-term earnings and annual shareholder value added represented by such measures as economic value added (EVA). Chapter 5 will show how EVA can be used to make the trade-offs on the efficient frontier.

This chapter has shown how the dialogue process initially used to develop and evaluate alternatives at the business-unit level can be applied at the level of corporate portfolio strategy. This is far different than simply adding up the strategies of the individual business units and then discovering that they either exceed corporate resources or fail to support corporate goals. The virtue of the process is to identify strategies with the best trade-offs between corporate goals—in the case of the example company, between shareholder value and current earnings. This is the same trade-off that many executives face and attempt to manage every day.

The best strategies define the efficient frontier. Unless you know where that frontier is for a particular business, it is impossible to know whether you are doing the best you can do for shareholders. Unfortunately, few corporations can define their efficient frontiers or where their current strategies stand relative to them.

The efficient frontier is a bit like the western frontier confronted by the early European settlers of North America. It represents the border between what we know and what we can envision. In British America, that frontier was initially defined by the first land clearings carved out of the forests that covered the Atlantic coastline. No one understood what lay beyond. Over time, knowledge gathered by surveyors, hunters, traders, and explorers expanded that initial frontier, first to the Appalachian Mountains, then to the Mississippi River and beyond.

In business, you can continue to expand the frontier of shareholder value to the extent that you can find superior alternatives to your current strategies. Finding these alternatives is the subject of Chapter 4.

4

Getting Alternatives That Create Value

Alternative strategies are the foundation on which portfolio companies and their business units build value. The CPG case in Chapter 3 demonstrated how a good set of alternatives can transform the future of a company. Unfortunately, strategic planning generally fails to bring good actionable alternatives to the attention of senior decision makers. More often than not, it serves up a set of variations on existing product lines and strategies. Although these may provide incremental growth and stability of earnings, they are incapable of renewing the business or obtaining major increases in corporate value. Lacking a powerful set of alternatives, the corporation is unlikely to find its way to the efficient frontier.

This chapter explains the causes of the alternatives problem and how they can be remedied. Those causes include the following:

- Organizational incentives discourage managers from championing alternative strategies; instead, they put managers' necks in the proverbial noose.
- Risks are confronted at the level of the business unit or the individual manager, not at the level of the corporation as a whole.
- The strategy development process is incapable of creating alternatives.
- The operational culture that dominates most organizations is more inclined to action than to creative thinking about new approaches to the business.

INCENTIVES THAT DISCOURAGE ALTERNATIVES

Big corporations spend lots of time and money trying to fine-tune performance-incentive programs that purport to align the interests of employees with those of the enterprise and its shareholders. In most cases, however, these incentives positively discourage the serious consideration of risky alternatives. To understand how, consider the following disguised situation encountered by my colleagues at a Fortune 100 corporation.[1]

The strategy development team of "XYZ Corporation," which included consulting personnel from Navigant, was making its final presentation to the CEO. The team had a great story to tell. Its members had spent six months developing alternative strategies for each of the corporation's operational groups: for the purpose of this story, engines, electronic components, advanced components, facilities management, dealer network services, and consumables. They had arrived at these strategies from intensive brainstorming and analysis by cross-functional teams within each operating group. The value range for each alternative strategy was measured in terms of its NPV and contrasted with an objective measurement of the company's current long-range plan for each division. These were presented to the CEO in graphic form, shown here as Figure 4.1.

Figure 4.1 shows the corporation's long-range plan (LRP) for each operating group, along with one or more of the best alternative strategies for these same groups. The bars shown in the figure represent the

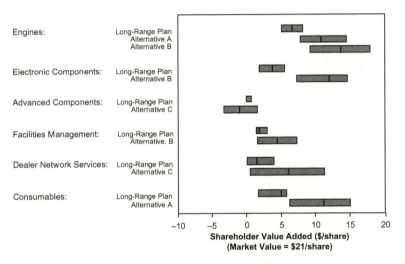

Figure 4.1 Strategic alternatives for XYZ Corporation.
Source: Navigant Consulting, Inc.

range of shareholder value added by each strategy in terms of dollars per share. As in previous chapters that have shown this format, there is an estimated 10 percent likelihood that the actual value will be less than the left edge of each bar and an estimated 10 percent likelihood that the actual value will be more than the right edge of each bar. In other words, 80 percent of the outcomes will fall somewhere within each bar. The longer the bar, the greater the range of possible outcomes—that is, the greater the uncertainty of the strategy's eventual results.

The line near the middle of each bar is the expected (probability-weighted) value of the stated strategy. For example, the expected value of the current (LRP) strategy for the engines group adds about $7 per share with only a 10 percent chance that it could be less than $5 per share and a 10 percent chance it would be greater than $8 per share. However, alternative A for the engine group has an expected value of $11 per share and only a very small chance of producing an outcome worse than the long-range plan. Alternative B appears even better; its expected value to the corporation is nearly $13.50 per share, and its worst-case scenario is slightly better than the best-case scenario for the engine group's current strategy. In fact, alternative B is a no-brainer that increases the value of the company an expected $6.50 per share.

Alternative B for the electronic-components group should be another no-brainer for corporate decision makers. Similarly, all the alternatives look better than the current strategy for facilities management, dealer network services, and consumables. In the case of dealer network services, alternative C does add a good deal of risk, but it also adds about $4.50 per share on an expected value basis, and the low end is still slightly better than the current strategy.

Only in the advanced-components group is the current strategy clearly better than the best alternative that the team could muster, which was represented in its presentation as alternative C. This alternative would actually *reduce* the expected value of the business.

By just about any measure, this team's presentation should have made the corporation's CEO the happiest businessperson on the planet; it had just presented him with an opportunity to more than double the future value of the company. However, and to the amazement of all concerned, he responded with a verbal tongue lashing. The CEO stood up and demanded to know why he and senior management had not seen these alternatives before. "Our long-range plan—the one we've been pursuing for the past few years—is supposed to reflect the best options available to this corporation. Now suddenly, as if by magic, you're telling me that we have new and better opportunities capable of doubling the value of our business. And, so I'm told, these opportunities are based on ideas that come from our own people—which is to say that they have been lying around under your noses for all this time. Why weren't these brought to my attention? Have you people been sandbagging me with our long-term plan?" (Sandbagging is the deliberate act of setting low, easily achievable targets).

The team members were momentarily speechless. Minutes earlier, they had expected the CEO to be pleased with their work and to treat them as heroes. They now found themselves on the defensive, and each waited nervously for someone else to respond to the boss's tirade. Finally, one of the group vice presidents offered an explanation. The company's annual budgeting cycle and incentive programs, he explained, had systematically driven group managers to adopt the conservative, low value-added strategies that collectively made up the company's long-term plan.

"We are all rewarded for performance against budget," he told the CEO. "Every year the corporation demands more of everything: more cash, higher return on investment, and more profits than the year before. Investments are expected to pay off quickly, and there's very little patience for long-term projects."

The vice president further explained, "We are judged as if risk did not exist, and if we even mention it, we are accused of making excuses. The company's attitude seems to be that good managers should make risk go away. So why should anybody be surprised when people in this company stay away from risky projects? Unfortunately, most of the high-value alternatives in any of our operating groups are riskier than the long-term plan. The figure makes that clear."

"Until now," he continued, "we haven't seriously pursued many of these riskier alternatives for the simple reason that we cannot guarantee results. And the finance people want us to sign in blood that 'This is what I can deliver.' The last time they asked me to give them a number for the annual contribution of my group, I said 'between thirty million and fifty-two million.' They looked at me as though I was from outer space and said, 'No, we want to know what you can *commit* to.'"

The environment described by the vice president suggests a clear misalignment between the interests of the corporation and its managers, one that can be observed all too often. The corporation has every incentive to maximize the value it creates for shareholders, but the managers on whom it depends are incented to march to a different drum. Their interests are not served by maximizing value but in "making their numbers," and the surest way to do this is to pursue strategies that offer the greatest certainty—usually the low-value strategies.

In the end, shareholder value is not driven by CEOs but by dozens of managers busily making their numbers. These managers, and the incentives that shape their behavior, set the tone for the corporation as a whole and determine its ultimate performance.

Back at XYZ Corporation and its angry CEO, once the problem of perverse incentives was aired, he and his managers could move ahead, creating a set of uniquely different portfolios based on the LRP and the alternative group plans developed by the strategy teams. The presentation then continued with the efficient frontier, shown in Figure 4.2. The figure indicates that the highest-value portfolio of alternatives (portfolio A) would diminish current earnings by approximately 17 cents a share. The NPV of the company, however, would more than double! The CEO made his decision: "I don't think I could persuade the stock analysts and big investors that taking that kind of hit on current earnings would pay off later. However, I could sell portfolio B—it raises long-term share value by almost as much at a cost of only about 7 cents in current earnings. And I know where to get the 7 cents per share—we can take it out of our corporate overheads and still deliver all of the value associated with portfolio B."

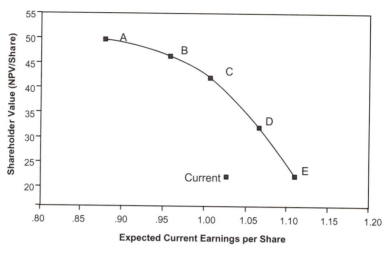

Figure 4.2 The efficient frontier for XYZ Corporation.

INDIVIDUAL VERSUS CORPORATE RISK

The incentive problem, as just illustrated, is related to risk—career risk in particular. The fear factor of an individual faced with a 40 percent chance of failure on a single roll of the dice is clearly much different than the fear factor of a large organization that has dozens of opportunities to roll the dice—especially if the cost of failure is high. The individual in this case has the odds slightly in his or her favor, but an unfortunate roll may be disastrous (demotion, loss of bonus, or loss of employment). The corporation, on the other hand, has the law of large numbers on its side: It can diversify its risks over many separate activities. As a result, it is likely to get an outcome that reflects the underlying probability. The lesson is this: *Corporations can tolerate higher risk levels than can their individual managers or their individual business units.*

Unfortunately, most organizations put the risk squarely on the shoulders of individual managers, with the result that the managers will only pursue projects that match their personal risk-comfort level, which may be pitifully low. As an example, consider a situation in which a general manager has a choice between two strategies: conservative growth and market leadership. Figure 4.3 illustrates this choice in a decision tree.

If the manager elects the market-leadership strategy, there is a 60 percent chance of success and a 40 percent chance of failure. To make the decision more complicated, the conservative growth strategy will generate $8 million more cash flow next year than the previous year and add an additional penny to earnings. The market-leadership strategy will actually re-

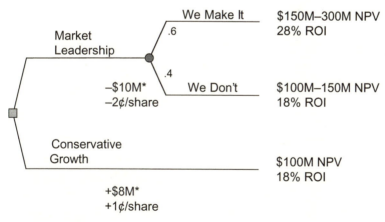

Figure 4.3 Choosing between conservative growth and market leadership.

duce cash flow by \$10 million next year and reduce the incremental contribution to corporate earnings by two cents a share. But notice that, even if this manager selects the market-leadership position and does not make it (a 40 percent probability), the corporation is no worse off than it was with conservative growth in terms of shareholder value.

For the manager in this example, going for the obvious best alternative is personally very risky, given the 60/40 probabilities and the fact that he gets to roll the dice just once. Most companies would only support investment in the market-leadership agenda if this general manager promised success (which would be foolish for him to do). Anything less, and senior management would say, "Jones won't commit and seems unsure about this program of his. He clearly has doubts. So, if he won't commit to it, why should we?" Statistically, the 60/40 probability shouldn't make the corporation as nervous as the manager. After all, it has many irons in the fire at once. Some will succeed and some will fail. But if the overall odds are favorable, the law of large numbers should put the corporation in the winning column.

So in the end, the corporation's demand for certainty backfires. It passes up a 60 percent chance of increasing its total value by \$50 to \$200 million so that a particular manager doesn't risk losing his \$140,000-per-year job. Does this seem like a perverse trade-off?

Corporate policies conspire against value-seeking managers in yet another way. Corporations often renege on their investment commitments even as they hold managers to theirs. To illustrate, let's return to the market-leadership–versus–conservative-growth choice just discussed. Let's suppose that Manager

Jones—despite his company's perverse incentives—does the right thing and says, "Yes, I'll commit to success with the market-leadership strategy." In return the company agrees to put the implementation resources into the budget. But next year, the financial people say, "Jones, we've had a bad year overall, so we need to cut everyone's budget by 15 percent, including yours." Jones is now in a double bind. If he had only a 60 percent chance of success with full funding, what are his odds of success after a funding cutback? His chance of market-leadership success is now probably approaching zero.

Jones was a good corporate soldier the first time around. If somehow he manages to survive, he will certainly play the game differently in the future; he will follow low-risk strategies that give him a better chance of making his numbers (and his raise, bonus, and promotion). In its perverse way, the company's incentives will produce exactly what it hopes to avoid: low-value creation.

A Real Managerial Solution

Fortunately, there are practical managerial solutions to the problem of getting good alternatives:

- A dialogue process that facilitates measurement and communication of risk, risk sharing across all levels of the organization, and a culture of trust.
- Incentives that support prudent risk taking.
- Strategy-driven budgets.

The Dialogue Process

The dialogue process provides the essential communication required to understand and share risks. Assessing the business situation and the risks of the current strategy (step 1 of the process, outlined in chapter 2) helps the business unit and the corporation understand the challenges that demand the consideration of risky alternatives. Step 2, development of creative alternatives, gives management confidence that alternatives are available (they always are) and that all the feasible options have been explored. Measurement of the potential risk and return of the alternatives (step 3) provides the essential base for comparing alternatives. At step 4, the corporate management team must commit to a decision and allocate the resources. In doing so, the team joins the business unit in committing to and sharing the risks of its choice.

When senior management comes to grips with risk in this way, corporate-level risk tolerance is applied to strategic business-unit decisions. This is an important change from conventional practice because *the corporation as a whole can support a higher level of risk than can the individual business unit or the individual manager.* To do otherwise is to practically guarantee excessive conservatism in important decisions and by extension, the pursuit of low-return strategies.

The creation of alternatives requires a culture of trust, which the dialogue process promotes. Much has been written about the nature of effective corporate culture and how it can be sustained. In *The Individualized Corporation*, Sumantra Ghoshal and Christopher Bartlett identify three elements of creating a trust-based culture:[2]

1. Transparency and openness.
2. Fairness and equity.
3. Shared organizational values.

The dialogue process supports all three, as many organizations have reported.[3] Good dialogue is naturally transparent and open. As it goes through the process, the organization creates a clear understanding of its business challenges its alternatives, and how its alternatives have been evaluated. Fairness and equity is baked into the process when each alternative is evaluated in the same way. The dialogue process gives senior managers a practical tool for communicating the values of the organizations and for others to pass them around. Every review meeting is an opportunity to communicate the organization's values and to receive feedback.

Incentive Systems That Support Prudent Risk Taking

One can find formal incentive systems for encouraging risk taking in many organizations. This is particularly true for companies in the oil exploration and pharmaceuticals industries, where risks must be taken routinely to renew asset portfolios.[4]

Effective incentive programs focus on the long term because risky business strategies and the many managerial decisions that support them must be allowed plenty of time to play themselves out. Incentive programs should focus on changes in shareholder value and economic value added over a number of years.[5] Although there may be no perfect incentive system, those that work well have a long-term perspective and take into account controllable and uncontrollable factors that management faces. They also share risks across the organization.

Strategy-Driven Budgets

Once a corporation and its senior managers commit to a strategy, that commitment must be reflected in operating budgets and the allocation of resources. The strategic decisions taken in step 4, decide among alternatives, must drive the annual budget. Thus selection of strategy becomes both a top down and a bottom up committment. Careful measurement of the efficient frontier permits management to make the choice of strategy drive the budget process. Those charged with implementing the strategy can then focus on the difficult work ahead and not on continual internal challenges and obstacles. Chapter 9 spells out a process for managing a smooth transition between decision making, strategy implementation, and operations.

THE STRATEGY-DEVELOPMENT PROCESS

Although most businesspeople agree that they need to consider alternatives, decision makers are all too often served up a thin menu of variations on the current strategy. Because they do not differ significantly from the current strategy, however, they are not real alternatives. The single greatest cause of this failure is a flaw in the process that strategists follow: Participants in the strategy-development process are asked to develop alternatives and evaluate them *at the same time.* Unfortunately, the human mind is seldom capable of being creative and analytical at the same time. The critical faculties required for analysis seem to carry the mind along channels that are incompatible with creative thinking. Analysis is concerned with identifying weaknesses, flaws, and relationships between elements; in contrast, creativity requires going beyond perceived boundaries, looking at things in new ways, building on existing ideas, and seeing how separate technologies can be brought together in new and useful forms. Experts in creativity, such as Edward De Bono, emphasize that most people get trapped in patterns of thought, and that creativity requires breaking those patterns (lateral thinking) and adopting new mental frameworks through which to approach the perceived problem.[6] Analytic procedures do just the opposite.

It is not surprising that, since the time of H.G. Wells, science-fiction writers have anticipated many of today's technological developments, both on earth and in space. Unfettered by analytical concerns of how these could actually be made to work, such creative minds paint pictures of possible new worlds and ways in which people might live in them. When Arthur C. Clarke created the dramatic events in the 1968 movie *2001: A Space Odyssey*, he probably had only the vaguest notion of how an orbiting space station could be built. Unencumbered by the need to work out every detail, he was free to sketch in broad strokes and images how humans would live and work in space, and through his plot and characters, he portrayed the conflicts they would encounter in that new and unexplored environment. Had Clarke felt compelled to work out every technical detail as he created his vision of the future, he would never have completed his work.

The dialogue process described in Chapter 2 deliberately separates creative and analytical tasks. Business assessment, the development of alternatives, and evaluation of alternatives are approached in three distinct stages. A separate step for alternative development permits people to be creative, to momentarily suspend judgment about what will and will not work, and to focus on the real challenges facing the business.

Arriving at creative alternatives is a process of developing and combining creative ideas into coherent alternative strategies with a consistent set of objectives and rationale. Strategy tables like the one shown in Table 4.1 and in Chapter 3 provide one practical mechanism that people can use to accomplish this.

For MegaPharma, one of the companies profiled in Chapter 3, Table 4.1 for the pharmaceutical business unit was the product of many idea-generation sessions in which participants sought to identify the strategic options available to their worldwide business. They combined a number of ideas into actionable alternatives that then were used to develop the MegaPharma portfolio strategy. Although the actual table developed by this business unit was considerably more complicated than the one shown here, this table still indicates that the team explored a wide range of possible options for each part of the business. The alternatives shown in Table 4.1 could never have been developed if the business unit strategy team had attempted to evaluate the details of each idea as it was raised.

Although some creative breakthroughs can be attributed to a stroke of genius, more often than not they result from the virtues of patience and persistence. No great inventor exemplifies those virtues better than "The Wizard of Menlo Park," Thomas Edison, who is credited with no less than 1,043 patents. Edison

Table 4.1 MegaPharma pharmaceutical business unit strategy table.

Strategy	International Focus	Domestic Marketing	Licensing and Joint Ventures	Generics	R&D Strategy
Short-term profit improvement Current	Worldwide presence	Maintain current sales force levels	Out-licensing limited to low-potential drugs and focused in-licensing with joint research agreements	Stay out and promote trademark to prevent erosion	Current Concentrate on key product classes
Focused reallocation	Build critical sales force mass in top 12 countries	Expand sales force to maintain current office-based coverage and increased hospital and key physician coverage	Aggressive out-licensing to achieve foreign potential and in-licensing to add domestic products	Selectively enter to use manufacturing capacity	Aggressively license to exploit strengths
Joint venture and license focus	Build, acquire companies, or joint venture to build critical mass in Germany, Japan, etc.	Maintain current sales force levels and increase non-sales promotion	Aggressive licensing and key joint venture	Cautious entry strategy based on marketing strength	
Broad-based expansion	Acquire company in Germany; out-licence in Japan, etc.				

was a great synthesizer of ideas—his own and others. Once he was on to something, he was tireless in its pursuit. His development of the first practical incandescent light bulb (the "electric candle," as he called it)—and the system of generators, sockets, and power distribution on which its success depended—is emblematic of his style.

Edison first saw a demonstration of electric arc lighting in 1878 in the workshop of another inventor, William Wallace, and quickly foresaw the commercial potential of electric lighting and in no time reckoned that it would be feasible to illuminate most of lower Manhattan with Wallace's dynamo and one 500-horsepower engine. Edison envisioned electric wires under the streets of New York, snaking through the tubing then used to bring gas into shops and homes for the same purpose.[7] But arc lighting was inappropriate for most indoor applications, so Edison set about finding "a candle that will give a pleasant light, not too intense, which can be turned on or off as easily as gas [and at] a trifling cost compared with that of gas."[8] This vision of the lighting business preceded a full year of laborious experimentation (testing several hundred filaments) and developmental work that produced his first operating prototype.

Edison's lighting innovations created one of the world's greatest corporations, General Electric. However, the inventor enjoyed at the time one of the luxuries of the entrepreneur: the ability to think freely about *possibilities,* unconstrained by the need to justify his thoughts to screening committees and financial analysts and other practical folk. Such creative speculation is more difficult in the modern corporate environment, but it remains as necessary for progress and renewal as in Edison's day and, as then, should be separated from analysis.

HOW OPERATIONAL CULTURES DISCOURAGE ALTERNATIVES

All successful companies develop strong operational cultures. These cultures are necessary when products must be built and shipped, when people must be hired, trained, and supervised, and when decisions must be made. Operational skills are essential for any manager who hopes to get ahead. However, the habits of people who create and develop good strategic alternatives are very different than those developed by good operating managers. One thinks, the other acts. One finds a path to the future, the other pursues the path vigorously. When an organization is dominated by operations and by executives who have risen to the top because of their operational skills, the culture of *doing* prevails; the organization directs little energy toward questioning the current strategy. Strategy becomes "what we do around here," and everyone's attention is on "doing what we do better." Alternatives to "what we do" aren't particularly welcomed. In a strong operating culture, people who dwell on alternatives are viewed as indecisive and ineffective.

Countless corporations have become operationally powerful but strategically weak, and with adverse consequences; IBM in the heyday of the mainframe computer provides a classic example. During the 1960s and 1970s, IBM built a market share of nearly 80 percent through superior R&D, marketing, and manufacturing. In the early 1980s, however, the market began to shift. Unfortunately, IBM's mainframe culture swamped its initial strategies to accommodate the shift toward smaller and more open systems.

Nor are operational cultures adept at dealing with strategic risks. Operational people are used to dealing with uncertainty in tactical situations. They usually recognize poor operational decisions quickly and in time to alter them with a minimum of damage. Strategic decisions, in contrast, call for major resource commitments over long periods. The outcomes of these decisions often cannot be known for years, and course corrections may be difficult or impossible. Few operational people have training or experience in dealing with strategic risks, and what people are not comfortable in dealing with, they tend to avoid or ignore.

People who seek alternatives in an operations-driven culture must also overcome a formidable number of idea killers. Common idea killers include the following:

- That's against company policy.
- Management will never sign off on it.
- That's not in our area of responsibility.
- Somebody's already tried that.
- It won't fly in our industry.
- Let's meet on that someday.
- Leave it with me— I'll work on it.
- We're not ready for that.
- It'll cannibalize our other products.
- Yes, but ...
- It won't sell in Peoria.
- Put it down on one sheet of paper.
- That creates as many problems as it solves.
- You can't argue with success.
- We'll never have time.
- Be more realistic.
- Great idea, but not for us.
- We need something more exciting.
- What will our customers think?
- That only solves half the problem.
- That would step on too many toes.
- We are on internet time.

Many people can tell you what is wrong with an idea, but few can find what is good in an idea and build on it. In some corporations, every idea is met with an idea killer. When this happens, only the most forceful individuals can be heard. What idea killers does your organization use?

Although the barriers to good strategic alternatives are many, the future prosperity of the corporation inevitably depends on overcoming them. Few businesses can grow by simply following their current strategies, even when those strategies have resulted in past success. Almost by definition, doing the same thing will produce—*at best*—the same result. To grow and prosper in a changing world, corporations have to do something different. Therein lies the power of strategic alternatives to create value.

5

Measuring a Portfolio's Annual Value Contribution

The previous chapters have shown how alternative strategies can be evaluated in terms of their total contributions to shareholder value. Net present value is the operative metric. This value will accrue to shareholders over some period of time—shorter for some strategies, longer for others. Not yet addressed is an issue that affects every executive and manager with profit-loss responsibility: how the NPV of alternative strategies be reflected in the market value of their share prices this year, next year, and in subsequent years. Joel Stern and G Bennett Stewart call this Economic Value Added (EVA).[1] In a nutshell, EVA describes the earnings produced by a corporation over and above its cost of capital on an annual basis.

There are two practical reasons for wanting to understand the annual shareholder value of alternative strategies. The first is that the conventional metric of company annual performance—accounting-based earnings—is terribly flawed. In many cases, accounting-based earnings is a poor indicator of *true* economic value, and decision makers who take earnings at face value are likely to choose strategies that are clearly inferior paths to increased shareholder wealth. They may even decrease value systematically. To understand why, consider the decision choice posed in the treatment of the efficient frontier in Chapter 3. There, executives of CPG, the example company, had to choose between a continuum of alternative strategies that held forth greater short-term earnings on the one hand and a higher NPV for the company on the other. This is a painful choice, and in my experience, one that confronts executives of *every* expense-driven company—to go for the short-term payoff (and keep their jobs and get their bonuses) or to do what is clearly best for shareholders in the long run. It is also a false choice in most instances. The short-term benefits on one end of the efficient frontier are generally illusions created by accounting conventions. Viewing the trade-off through the lenses of EVA, decision makers can filter out these illusions. In most cases, they will see that the long-term best alternatives are also best for shareholders (and the company's stock price) in the short term as well.

The second reason for determining the EVA of a strategy is its usefulness in communicating effectively with investors and employees. The investment community has begun to appreciate the difference between corporate earnings and true economic value. Thus, the executive who can communicate a long-term strategy in terms of annual additions to shareholder value has a good chance of seeing the NPV of that strategy reflected in the share price of their company's stock. Employees, too, need to understand how their efforts contribute to the true wealth of the corporation on a year-by-year basis. Once they see this, they can better link their everyday activities to the interests of shareholders. Linking the daily activities of employees is not as difficult as it seems if the business has a clear strategy and understands what drives the shareholder value of the strategy. If one expands the sensitivity analysis discussed in Chapter 2 (see Figure 2.4) to include the controllable and partially controllable factors that affect the business, it can be used to focus employees on the measures for which they are responsible.

THE PROBLEM OF ACCOUNTING-BASED EARNINGS

Most businesspeople and academics subscribe to the view that the NPV of future cash flows of a business equals its shareholder value. Further, nearly all authorities agree that *free cash flow* is the cash flow that matters. Free cash flow is the cash from operations that is available for potential distribution to lenders and shareholders. In determining the NPV of this free cash flow, the appropriate discount rate is the firm's weighted average cost of capital (WACC), including debt and equity. Of course, the cost of capital for debt must be adjusted downward to reflect the fact that it is tax deductible. A number of excellent books describe the procedures for calculating NPV.[2]

As important as NPV is to the assessment of a business, the investor will search in vain through annual reports for this figure. The NPV figures that appear in annual reports are buried in footnotes and are used to value relatively limited classes of assets or liabilities, such as leases. Corporations would be foolish to publish such numbers for the entire business (at least in the United States, the land of lawyers) for fear that any projected values not realized would provoke a flurry of shareholder suits!

In the absence of NPV estimates for companies, analysts and investors have used price-to-earnings (P/E) ratios to explain how the stock market values different companies. They look at last year's earnings and then try to project them forward one or more years, in each case assigning a multiple of each dollar of earnings. For example, if the market is currently paying an average of $25 per share for each current dollar of earnings for companies in the pharmaceutical business, analysts interested in the future value of XYZ Pharmaceuticals will project the company's earnings and multiply it by 25.

Unfortunately, as a guide to perceived value, the P/E ratio is notoriously fickle. First, the multiple assigned to a given company or the market in general fluctuates with the mood of investors and the larger economic environment. For instance, in mid-1998 companies in the Standard & Poor's 500 were, on average, trading at over 20 times current earnings—high by historical standards. During the early stages of a bear market, these same companies may be trading at 12 to 15 times current earning—even those whose fortunes continue to expand.[3]

If the NPV of free cash flow is the best measure of shareholder value, how can investors *see* its impact on an annual basis? One approach is to look at annual free cash flow. But there is a better measure: EVA. Economic value added is what managers and investors should keep their eyes on. The true value of a company in the marketplace is generally obscured by the measurement of earnings under generally accepted accounting principals (GAAP). For example, when a company builds a manufacturing plant, it can expect to receive value from its productive capacity for many years. The response of the accountants (as codified by GAAP) is to capitalize the plant and depreciate a fraction of its value during each year of the useful life of the plant. Thus, a fraction of the capital cost of building the plant is used to reduce reported earnings. Capitalizing plant and equipment makes much sense, but this sensible approach is not extended to investments in other assets or activities that, like the manufacturing plant, also create shareholder value. The work that goes into new-product development, for example, can create tremendous value. Indeed, the fortunes of companies like Pfizer, Microsoft, Intel, and many others are more driven by what occurs in R&D laboratories than what happens in factories. In a technology-driven age, machinery and bricks and mortar count for less and less. Yet accounting principles require that R&D investments be *expensed*—that is, charged against earning—in the year in which they are incurred, throwing a heavy burden on the bottom line. For a pharmaceutical company, this means that R&D activities that will contribute substantial shareholder value many years from now must be counted against current earnings.

Investment in R&D is not the only class of expenditures that produce value far beyond the year in which they occur. Advertising and promotion aimed at creating brand equity do the same. Given the inadequacies of accounting-based earnings, financial analysts have looked elsewhere for reliable measures of company value: cash flow, free cash flow, and earnings before interest, taxes, depreciation, and amortization (EBITDA). Unfortunately, each of these measures emerges from the same flawed root: operating earnings as determined by GAAP.

Analysts have also viewed return on capital as a promising alternative. Since the 1960s, businesspeople and financial analysts have been aware of a relationship between the market value of their companies, the cost of capital, and their returns on capital investments. In response, numerous ratio measures such as return on equity (ROE), return on investment (ROI), and return on net assets (RONA) have been employed to measure the return on capital. Some of these measures are demonstrably superior to others, but all suffer from a common problem—they ignore the size and growth of the enterprise and tempt managers to shift resources to activities or business units with the highest ratio. For example, an inexperienced manager might say, "Why are we focusing resources on our mass-market consumer goods, which have only a 15 percent ROI, while our small specialty-goods division is pumping out a 30 percent ROI?" The ratio may be absolutely superior, but the absolute dollars of shareholder value added by the mass-market unit may be much larger because of its much greater volume.

It is arguable that the use of such ratio measures as ROI in the late 1960s and 1970s caused many U.S. and European companies to cede large but lower-ratio businesses to their foreign competitors. Swiss watchmakers, for example, retreated from the low- to mid-range watch market, where margins were puny, as Asian competitors flooded stores with cheap, but reliable, time pieces. The ROI on the Swiss premium brands was quite high, and their retail prices were stratospheric.

Unfortunately, sales volume at the top-of-the-market pyramid was miniscule (some 3 million units per year) compared to the low- and mid-range markets (450 million and 42 million units per year, respectively), and the revenues and earnings of Swiss watchmakers collapsed. Only the innovation of the Swatch watch—a simple but elegantly designed, low-priced item that sold in huge volumes—stemmed the tide.[4]

Consider where Hewlett-Packard would be if it had continued to focus only on its test-and-measurement business, where margins of 50 to 55 percent are achievable, and had not pursued opportunities in the mass printer market. Today, HP's printer business generates over three times the revenues of its test-and-measurement business while still maintaining a healthy 30 to 35 percent margin,[5] while the test-and-measurement business is being spun off.

ECONOMIC VALUE ADDED

Although the *return* on capital has been a major issue for executives and investors for years, the *cost* of capital to the firm has only recently been a matter of concern to the general business population. Not so many years ago, CEOs, corporate treasurers, and other financial managers were the only people who gave the cost of capital a thought. Down in the business units and functional departments, managers could not have cared less. Their performances were judged on criteria that totally ignored the price paid for the capital they used every day. Even the popular ROI performance metric considers only the *amount* of capital and not its cost. Capital was treated as a free good by just about everyone. Managers who sat atop billions-worth of capital equipment were evaluated on sales increases, contribution margins, and various return-on-assets metrics that simply failed to account for the cost of capital used in their operations. "My unit had another great year," they would crow, even though their corporations were paying millions for the capital tied up in their operations. In many cases, the shareholders would have been better off if these operations had been eliminated, their personnel reassigned, and the locked-up capital redirected to investments in government securities!

If the cost of capital was unappreciated in the past, its importance is now generally understood. Business people have come to recognize the cost of capital implicit in the operational performance of corporations and business units. The idea of reducing traditional metrics such as earnings or cash flow by a capital charge has become an increasingly popular approach to measuring the *true* economic contribution made by business units, departments, and individual managers each year. Economic value added accomplishes this and as a result does a better job of explaining how the stock market recognizes the buildup of NPV. Economic value added is defined as earnings minus the weighted cost of capital times the capital employed (EVA = E − WACC × CE, where E is the adjusted earnings, WACC is the weighted cost of capital, and CE is the capital employed). Note that the earnings and capital employed in the formula must be adjusted to reflect how actual economic value is created. At last count, over 160 potential adjustments to both the operating statement and balance sheet are needed to exactly calculate EVA. Fortunately, only a few of these adjustments are required for a specific business to reflect how it builds real shareholder value. The key is to focus on the handful of adjustments that materially impact shareholder value. Of course, these are different for different businesses and are reflected in their differing success templates.

Economic value added is a powerful tool for translating the buildup of corporate NPV into stock-market value because the discounted sum of EVA equals the NPV of the company. Economic value added and similar measures are useful in helping managers determine the amount of *actual*—not accounting—value being contributed to shareholder wealth during any given period by an operating unit or by the corporation as a whole.

But what about the value added by a particular strategy? To calculate EVA for a strategy, one must look at the success template of the business to see how the business creates actual wealth for shareholders. Simply put, a success template is that set of activities that makes it possible for a company to generate real wealth (as opposed to accounting profits). The success template for a pharmaceutical company, for example, includes (1) effective R&D, (2) a strong product pipeline, (3) excellence in manufacturing, and (4) promotion through a detail sales force whose goal is to convince doctors to prescribe their drugs. The following discussion considers just the fourth part of that success formula and how its promotional expenses should be handled.

Ideally, promotional costs that create lasting shareholder value should be capitalized. For example, the expenses associated with a pharmaceutical sales force that calls on doctors should be capitalized. This sales force provides doctors with a technical explanation of the use and benefits of a drug, but the sales people themselves take no orders. The doctors' prescriptions provide the sales. By convincing the doctors to pre-scribe, the sales force sets the doctors' prescription habits. And because these habits are slow to change, they represent lasting shareholder value for the phar-maceutical company. Nevertheless, GAAP requires that the drug company's investment in its sales force be *expensed*. (Generally accepted accounting principles are designed to be applied consistently and prudently by all kinds of companies. Economic value added needs to reflect how a specific company or industry will create value in the future.)

Fortunately, distortions caused by accounting con-ventions can be corrected easily. The only items in conventional financial statements that require adjust-ments are those that reflect how the business will build shareholder value in the future. All other correc-tions are purely academic, even though some financial analysts argue their merits with theological intensity. The future changes in EVA are what increase or de-crease the market value of any business.

Projecting Future Economic Value Added

The most common use of EVA by corporations today is for incentive compensation. Managers with profit and loss responsibility are finding that their bonuses are being tied to metrics that reduce their contribu-tions to corporatewide profits by a charge for the capi-tal they use. The concern at this point, however, is less with executive compensation than with how the value added by each alternative strategy will be recognized *annually* by shareholders. Because EVA measured in dollars is a better predictor of future share price than are P/E ratios, returns on capital or cash-flow multiples, management needs to be concerned with projecting the EVA of its portfolio strategy.

Before proceeding to the calculation, let's return to CPG, Inc., the company introduced in Chapter 3. It is a worldwide company with outstanding consumer brands. Companies like CPG typically build shareholder value through brand equity based on the following:

- Creating successful new products through R&D.
- Launching new products.
- Launching existing products in new markets.
- Advertising and promoting current products in current markets.
- Optimized pricing.
- Reducing cost in production and distribution.

Each of these initiatives requires a financial investment. In the case of its R&D investment, CPG finds that the average life of its investments is five years. That is to say, the products it develops through R&D enjoy, on average, a profitable market life of five years. But averages never tell the entire tale. Some new products (e.g., a "new and improved" version of buffered aspirin) are completed in a year or less and survive in the marketplace for only a year or two. Others have real staying power, representing an entirely new product type, and contribute to shareholder value for decades. Advil is such branded product. (The active ingredient in Advil, ibuprofen, was originally a prescription product, and Advil was introduced as an ibuprofen-based product.) However, for this example company, five years is the average.

To compute EVA, one has to capitalize CPG's investment in R&D in any given year and amortize it over the subsequent five years. Other costs should get the same treatment. The cost of launching a new product is represented in additional manufacturing capacity and advertising associated with the product launch. The additional investment in manufacturing is already properly handled (capitalized) by GAAP, but the additional advertising expense is not.

In truth, some advertising costs should be expensed in the year incurred because they generate sales in the year in which the advertising is conducted. For CPG, advertising costs build brand equity. Consumers make repeat purchases over long periods if they like a product, assuming that the product is priced competitively, and so on. If consumers like a product, it acquires a franchise. These franchises are usually multiyear. This would dictate that franchise-building costs be capitalized. In the case of this consumer packaged-goods company, promotional expenses are primarily slotting fees and other expenses associated with getting and keeping its products properly displayed on the shelf; these costs should not be capitalized because they are incurred annually and do not build lasting shareholder value.

If advertising builds brand equity, the problem becomes determining to what extent and how rapidly brand equity declines. Studies conducted by Navigant Consulting indicate that, for CPG, the value of brand equity declines at a rate of 30 percent per year. This rate varies, of course, with the product in question. Every consumer-product category appears to have a particular depreciation rate. In accounting terms, this means that advertising should be capitalized and then depreciated at a constant declining balance rate.

Table 5.1 illustrates how capitalizing value-building expenses works in practice. This table shows the operating income statement and balance sheet of CPG. The

Table 5.1 Financial statements for CPG, Inc.

Operating Statement		
Description	Current ($ millions)	Revised ($ millions)
Sales	6,243	6,243
Cost of goods sold	2,283	2,283
Advertising	894	672
Selling and promotion	1,251	1,251
Administration	543	543
R&D	153	112
Intangibles	54	0
Before-tax profit	1,065	1,382
Cash taxes	336	279
After-tax profit	729	1,103
Capital charge		671
Annual shareholder value added		433

Balance Sheet		
Description	Current ($ millions)	Revised ($ millions)
Current Assets	1,830	1,830
Net PP&E	1,008	1,008
Intangibles	2,100	0
Capitalized-Advertising	0	2,297
Capitalized R&D	0	454
Total Net Assets	4,938	5,589

first column for each (current) follows GAAP. The second column (revised) restates those numbers in terms of annual shareholder value added. The differences are striking. The first point of difference is in advertising expense in the operating statement, which decreases from $894 million to $672 million. Capitalized advertising on the balance sheet is zero under GAAP but $2,297 million when computed in terms of EVA. The $894 million advertising expense reflects the advertising spent during the year, whereas the $672 million expense reflects the amortization of advertising incurred during the fiscal year based on the capitalized advertising and the depreciation rate of 30 percent.

The next point of difference is the R&D expense on the operating statement. Under GAAP, R&D is $153 million versus $112 million in EVA. A look at the balance sheet explains the difference. With GAAP, all R&D in this industry must be expensed during the year incurred; for EVA, however, current-year R&D expenditures are capitalized and amortized over a five-year period. This results is capitalized R&D of $454 million versus zero following GAAP.

Intangibles represent another point of difference. Intangibles, including goodwill attributable to previous acquisitions, are reported on the GAAP operating statement but are neglected (in this case) when computing EVA. Similarly, the GAAP balance sheet shows $2,100 million in intangibles, an amount neglected on the EVA balance sheet. It is important to note that this intangible simplification has been made because the company is not looking at acquisitions going forward. A purist would argue that intangibles represent real capital that has been spent in the past and that needs to be properly adjusted in computing annual shareholder value added. However, because it does not influence CPG's choice of future strategy, one can neglect it.

Next, consider taxes. Taxes as reported in the GAAP operating statement are those accrued during the fiscal year and include both taxes that will be paid in the next year and deferred taxes. When computing EVA, however, one only cares about the *actual* cash tax payments made during the year. Therefore, the revised column utilizes $279 million to compute annual shareholder value added versus the reported taxes of $336 million.

The final point of difference is a capital charge, which needs to be considered in computing annual shareholder value added. The capital charge is determined by multiplying total net assets of $5,589 million on the balance sheet by the weighted average cost of capital—in the case of CPG, 12 percent. The result is a capital charge of $671 million. The after-tax profit minus the capital charge equals an annual shareholder value added of $433 million, 41 percent *less* than the $729 million profit reported by standard accounting.

BACK TO THE EFFICIENT FRONTIER

As discussed in Chapter 3, CPG had the efficient frontier shown in Figure 5.1. It indicates that short-term earnings decline as shareholder value increases. Although this seems paradoxical, it is because the company's more aggressive strategies require additional R&D and advertising expenditure to create shareholder value, both of which reduce reported earnings in the short term.

The trade-off between higher shareholder value in the long run and higher earnings in the short term

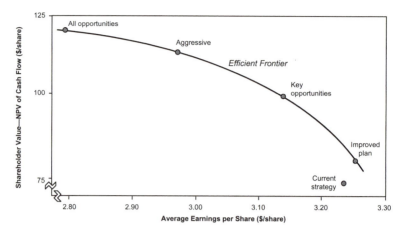

Figure 5.1 CPG's efficient frontier.

presents management with a difficult choice. Its overarching duty is to maximize the wealth of the shareholders, but any choice that reduces current earnings (and current share price) may be suicidal. If management were to focus solely on average short-term earnings per share, a constant price-to-earnings ratio of 23 would give the company a share price of $74.50 ($3.24 × 23) for the current strategy. In contrast, embarking on the all-opportunities strategy in Figure 5.1 would reduce share price to $64.40 ($2.80 × 23), even though this strategy builds the most long-term shareholder value.

Of course, shareholders generally look beyond short-term earnings to a company's long-term prospects for growth. To the extent that senior executives can communicate the long-term benefit of the more aggressive strategy to shareholders and the financial community, they will be allowed to pursue it. The company's stock may even be rewarded with a higher P/E ratio and, as a consequence, a higher share price.

To appreciate the decision more completely, consider Figure 5.2, which shows the earnings (after-tax profit) projections for the company under each of the five portfolio strategies, first discussed in Chapter 3. The current strategy has higher earnings in 1996 than any of the alternatives—even the improved plan— and continues to do so until 1999, after which all alternatives are superior to it. It could be argued that four years is a long time to wait to realize the value of a better strategy, especially when that higher value is not assured!

But how will investors recognize the buildup of shareholder value? If they look at EVA—and there is considerable evidence that they do—the company must do the same. Projecting each strategy's EVA forward over a seven-year period results in the picture shown in Figure 5.3. This projection is made through the procedure described in the previous section on capitalizing advertising and R&D expenditures, utilizing actual cash taxes paid in the year they are paid, neglecting intangibles, and subtracting a capital charge.

A striking difference occurs by shifting from simply projecting accounting-based profits to the EVA. As Figure 5.3 indicates, the current strategy produces the *least* EVA per year in *every* year! Even the improved-plan portfolio strategy is not very attractive. By 1997 the aggressive and key-opportunities strategies are clearly superior to the other alternatives and remain so until 2001 when the all-opportunities strategy takes the lead.

So what is a manager to do? It is important to emphasize that there is no right answer in selecting a portfolio strategy, nor is there a single right measure of shareholder value. Senior management must con-

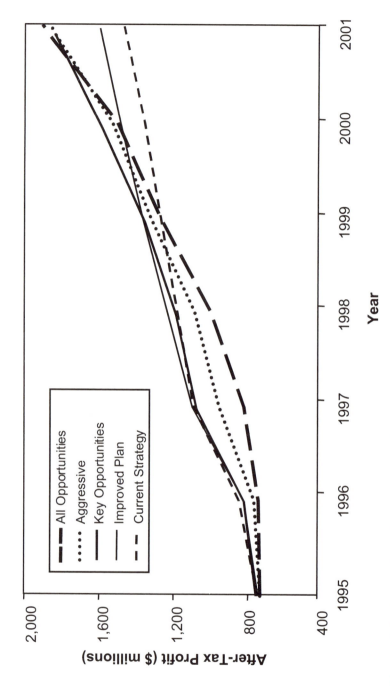

Figure 5.2 Conventional after-tax profits.

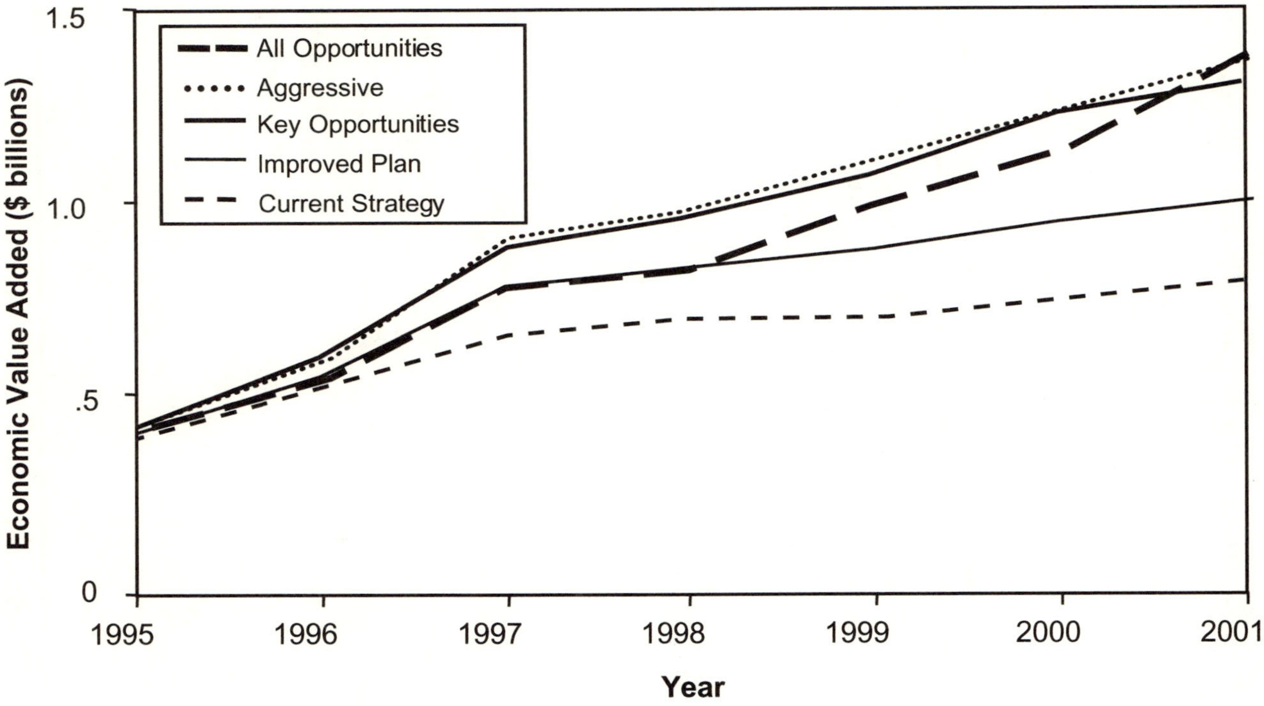

Figure 5.3 EVA values.

125

sider all the data—earnings, efficient frontiers, plus EVA—in making an informed judgment. The key is to consider business-unit and portfolio alternatives that add value. That is the real secret to portfolio strategy. Combining good alternatives with good methods of valuation creates the basis for making decisions that will dramatically increase corporate value.

As shown in Chapter 3, each of the alternative strategies available to our consumer-products company involves more risks than does the current strategy; however, none involves unacceptable risks. As a result, most corporate managers could elect either the key-opportunities or the aggressive strategy and still sleep well at night knowing that they have added over 30 to 50 percent to both short-term and long-term shareholder value.

6

Managing Success Templates and Business-Unit Life Cycles

There is much more to making multibusiness companies successful than correctly measuring shareholder value, operating on the efficient frontier, and using the dialogue process to expand the frontier. The executives and employees who run them must also understand and effectively manage the businesses in their portfolios. Do these businesses fit together? Are they focused on profitable markets and on activities at which the corporation is outstanding?

Prosperous multibusiness corporations operate through one or a few *success templates*. A success template is a figurative blueprint for making money. McDonald's found its success template in the fast-food hamburger restaurant. Over the years, it developed and perfected that money-making concept, taking it across North America and around the world. Staples has done the same in the field of office supplies (i.e., superstores with huge inventories and low prices); so has Intel, with a steady stream of cheaper and faster generations of microprocessors.

A success template has six elements:

1. The source of added value; the company's position in the value chain defines its source of added value.
2. The customers served by the company.
3. Products and/or services provided to customers.
4. The company's source of opportunities for growth and renewal.
5. Core competencies[1] (e.g., excellence in product development or marketing) and business strengths (e.g., patents or market leadership).
6. How the company protects its position against encroachment.

Figure 6.1 shows an example of a success template for the well-known Bell Yellow Pages. It contains each of the six elements.

No success template retains its potency forever. The success template is inexorably linked to the life cycle of the business. The typical business unit follows a course similar to the standard product life cycle with which most readers are familiar. This life cycle generally begins as a profitless or minimally profitable phase during which the new business and its products seek a place in the market. If successful, it enters a new phase of rapidly rising sales and growing profitability. A period of maturity and substantial profits is

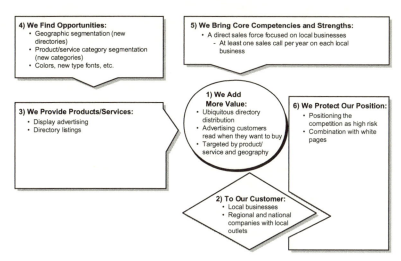

Figure 6.1 The Yellow Page's success template.

next. Then, in all likelihood, the business will experience declining sales and profits.

Each business unit in the corporate portfolio will likely be in a different phase of its cycle at any given time. One may be the mature phase, generating substantial profits. Another may be at the point of steep upward ascent, with customer adoption of its products or services growing rapidly. Yet another portfolio unit, one whose success template has lost its potency, may be in decline.

Business life cycles, such as the one shown in Figure 6.2, have distinct phases that may last for decades. The line in the figure represents sales during the different phases, which, in most cases, is a leading indicator of profits. The duration of these life cycles often lulls senior managers into complacency and weds them to strategies that are appropriate in one part of the life cycle but disastrous in another.

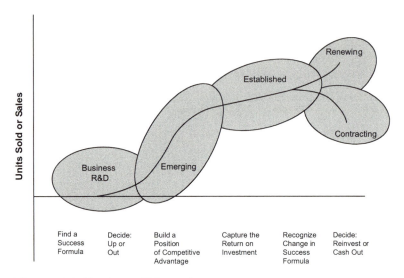

Figure 6.2 Business life cycle.

PHASE 1: BUSINESS R&D

The goal of management in the first phase, business R&D, is twofold: (1) to find a success template capable of propelling the business into the future, and (2) to kill off losers. A success template is a model for profitable enterprise and is best explained by example. Consider the case of Michael Dell, a relative latecomer to the personal-computer business. Dell was neither a technical innovator nor did he find new applications for computer hardware or software. Instead, he created and implemented a template for the direct marketing of PC hardware and software that attracted customers and confounded rivals.

Anyone who has dealt with Dell Computer Corporation is familiar with its approach to taking and fulfilling customer orders. Either by telephone or on the

Internet, the customer configures a PC that suits his or her unique needs: for example, a 330 megahertz Pentium machine with 64K RAM, 8 gigabits of hard-drive memory, a 20× CD drive, with a 17-inch color monitor, and so on, preloaded with Microsoft Windows and Office and other selected software. Dell quickly assembles this particular unit from a common set of components, loads it with the customer's choice of software, and rushes it to the loading dock. Less than a week after the order is placed, the semicustom-designed PC is at the customer's door and ready to go.

Dell's direct-business model is deceptively simple but is supported by a carefully crafted value chain that includes product design, hardware and software suppliers, component assembly, customer sales and service, a powerful customer-information system, and formidable logistics. By 1998 that high-tuned value chain of activities was generating almost $14 billion per year, making Dell the fastest-growing computer-systems provider on the planet. The company continues to blur the traditional lines in the value chain, moving toward what Dell calls *virtual integration.* In so doing, it has reduced the distance between customer and supplier, making Dell Computer the "IT department" for its corporate customers and not just another PC vendor.[2]

A brief analysis of just about any leading business will reveal the presence of a powerful success template, one that competitors can see but must struggle to replicate—and with no assurance of success. Long-term leaders manage to protect their success templates through trade secrets, a thicket of product or process patents, or by other means. The importance of this protection cannot be overemphasized.

PHASE 2: BUILDING COMPETITIVE
ADVANTAGE IN AN EMERGING BUSINESS

Once a potential success template is found, a company must use it to capture market share. This is the second phase, building a competitive advantage in an emerging business. Grabbing the lion's share of the market is the most effective way to gain competitive advantage and to make entry by competitors difficult if not impossible. In contrast, perhaps the most unforgivable sin in business is to create a market for others to exploit, as Litton Industries did with the microwave oven. Litton was one of the initial licensees of the microwave oven invented by Raytheon. In the 1970s, Litton used that license to open the door to a brand-new market but failed to improve the product to the point where every household could see the need to own one. This failure to aggressively exploit first-mover advantage opened the door to Asian companies that improved on the existing technology and, by the mid-1980s, had flooded the market with their less-expensive, more-popular models. Eventually, Litton—the company that pioneered the microwave market—was forced out of the business entirely.[3]

The faster the rate of product adoption in a market, the more critical it is to grab the number-one market position. The loss of IBM's early dominance in the PC industry underscores this point. Big Blue's skunk works in Boca Raton, Florida, gave it a commanding lead in the exploding new PC market. But the company made a fatal mistake. It brought that product line back into the IBM fold, where delays, product shortages, technology problems, and new models that were less than state-of-the-art (the ill-fated PS/2 being an example) gave clone makers of all stripes the opening they needed to carve up the new territory for themselves. Today, the business is dominated by companies that didn't even exist at the dawn of the PC age.

Why do innovators of a success template create a fast-growing market only to watch swifter competitors race past them with the same concept? In almost all cases, the reason is a failure to improve and innovate.

PHASE 3: CAPTURING THE RETURN ON THE ESTABLISHED BUSINESS

The third phase, capturing the return on the established business, coincides with broad market acceptance of the business concept. By this time, the first phase of customer adoption is over and the initial competitors are established. The contending businesses are usually still growing as they enter this stage, and a shakeout is often in process. Survivors continue to grow as they capture share and revenue from those that stumble. However, most find that forward progress is much tougher.

The computer mainframe market from the mid-1960s to the mid-1980s provides a classic example of phase 3. Many companies, including Burroughs, Univac, Control Data, and Honeywell, continued to vie with IBM for market share. The business was still growing and changing even though it was in its mature phase.

PHASE 4: DEVELOP A NEW SUCCESS TEMPLATE THROUGH BUSINESS R&D

One could call this fourth phase—developing new success templates through R&D—the *challenge phase* because the mature business left untended is bound to lose cash and profitability. Markets are saturated, and new and better substitutes appear. Even those that manage to hold the line on sales feel their profitability ebbing as competitors cut prices to keep production lines busy. What were once unique products and services are now commodities commanding commodity prices. Faced with this dismal situation, a company must either find a new success template capable of reinventing the business or accept contraction.

A new success template can take many forms. Here are just a few:

• *Industry consolidation.* In mature industries, a low-cost producer generally drives out competitors. Matsushita and others have accomplished this in television sets.

• *A radical change in distribution.* Staples, the office-supply superstore, represents a new success template in an otherwise moribund sector of the retail economy. Focusing on the small- to medium-sized business customers who typically make low-volume purchases at high prices from a local retailer, Staples brought a wide selection of office supplies, office furniture, and office equipment under one roof at discount prices.

Egghead Software's total abandonment of traditional brick-and-mortar retailing in favor of online sales provides another example, as it recognized the need to adopt a new success template or die. Faced with intense competition from megastores like Comp-USA, Egghead in early 1998 announced its intention to close all of its retail stores in favor of online sales through three Internet sites. As of this writing, the jury is still out on the wisdom of Egghead's move.

One would speculate that the current template for distributing automobiles via dealerships loaded with acres of inventory will also give way to a much different and more cost-efficient model unless legislation protects the current system.

• *A technological or product breakthrough.* For decades, sheet steel was made exclusively through a process that ran a thick block of white-hot steel through miles of milling machines and reheating furnaces. Step by step, this hugely capital-intensive process reduced the mattress-sized block into a thin roll of finished steel. When upstart Nucor Corporation successfully implemented a new process for pouring and milling a continuous ribbon of steel, cost per ton dropped like a rock, and the industry dramatically changed.

In the absence of a strategy for renewing the business, contraction is generally assured. Some established businesses can continue to grow as demographic increases enlarge the total market year by year, but fierce competition for these small increases makes this growth expensive.

A period of slow contractions can be quite profitable for some companies if the right strategy is pursued. For example, continuously downsizing and restructuring can be a successful strategy for preserving profitability. However, the wrong strategy in the challenge phase of the business life cycle, such as continuing to invest heavily in an obsolete business template, can trap the cash of the unwary. Many of the big U.S. steel producers continued to pour cash into their antiquated plants almost until the day they closed them.

One Company's
Changing Success Template

A business life cycle is best observed over a long period of time. Eastman Kodak Company, whose origins began more than a century ago, provides an excellent opportunity for this. It is a company that has found new success templates over the years, making self-renewal possible. Today, it stands again at the crossroads of renewal and decline, and its future will be determined by the ability of its managers to discover and implement a new success template.

Origins and Innovations

Modern film-based photography is a direct technical descendent of daguerreotype, an imaging technology developed in France during the late 1830s. Daguerreotype produced an image on chemically sensitized copper plates. Over the course of the nineteenth century, this imaging method gave way in turn to three important technical changes, each of which simplified the job of taking pictures, expanded the market, and spawned a new set of competitors:

- *Wet-plate photography.* Introduced in the mid-1850s, this method used colloidion-coated glass plates photosensitized with a silver nitrate solution just prior to exposure. The exposed plates produced excellent quality images; however, the major drawback of this method was that the plates needed immediate, on-the-spot development after exposure, requiring the photographer to have a darkroom and materials on-site.

- *Dry-plate photography.* Introduced in the late 1870s, this technology used glass plates coated with a gelatin-based photosensitive emulsion. These plates could be manufactured in advance and kept handy in lightproof packaging. Once exposed, the plates could be stored in lightproof cases for later development. As a medium, dry plates were a dramatic improvement over prior technology. As James Utterback has explained, dry-plate technology "made it possible to produce nonperishable photosensitive glass plates in factories, thus making photography less complicated, more convenient, and cheaper, due to large-scale production of one of its key components."[4]

- *Celluloid film photography.* As perfected by George Eastman and his chief chemist, Henry Reichenbach, in 1889, rolls of thin celluloid film made it possible to replace heavy, breakable glass plates, greatly simplifying picture taking and lowering its costs. Cameras could for the first time be made small and lightweight. Perhaps as important, film photography made it possible to separate the task of shooting pictures—something that amateurs could do—from the technical business of photo-development. This expanded the market by many orders of magnitude.

Prior to the development of celluloid film photography, taking pictures was the domain of professionals, requiring heavy, expensive equipment and training in the use of chemical processes. Few amateurs had the knowledge or dedication to produce their own photographs. In addition, photography was expensive. George Eastman's first photographic outfit cost him nearly a month's wages—and he was a successful banker!

In 1878, with financial backing from Harry Strong, a successful buggy-whip manufacturer, Eastman entered the business of producing dry plates and photographic supplies. (Yes, a buggy-whip manufacturer actually invested in a revolutionary new business!) At the time, this was a commodity business with plenty of competitors. Eastman, however, developed the glass-cleaning, stamping, ventilation, and coating equipment necessary to produce dry plates on a large scale. Thus, although the products of the Eastman Dry Plate Company differed little from those of its competitors, the company's superior process technology provided the success template it needed to grow and prosper until a new and more powerful concept was found (see Figure 6.3).

Process competencies and a set of distribution arrangements allowed Eastman to service international markets, a unique strategy for the U.S. photographic industry at the time. He traveled to England to patent his process there before he patented it in the United States.

The Growth Phase

Economic history is full of short-lived, one-product-wonder companies. Examples include Osborne Computer Company, developer of the first portable (luggable) computer, Visi Corporation, developer of Visicalc, the first spreadsheet program, and the Singer Freiden division of Singer Corporation, a calculator maker that briefly went into minicomputers, then quickly disappeared. Eastman's company could have

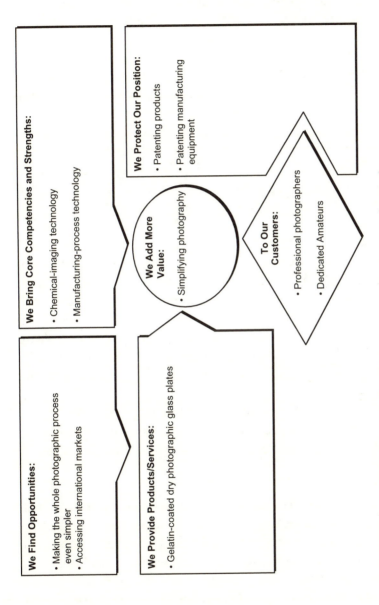

We Find Opportunities:
- Making the whole photographic process even simpler
- Accessing international markets

We Bring Core Competencies and Strengths:
- Chemical-imaging technology
- Manufacturing-process technology

We Provide Products/Services:
- Gelatin-coated dry photographic glass plates

We Add More Value:
- Simplifying photography

We Protect Our Position:
- Patenting products
- Patenting manufacturing equipment

To Our Customers:
- Professional photographers
- Dedicated Amateurs

Figure 6.3 Initial Eastman Dry Plate Company success formula.

been one of these, shouldered aside as the next wave of change swept through the industry. But Eastman was not content to bask in his success. Instead, he continued to explore ways to simplify the task of taking photographs. The innovation that made this possible was the replacement of coated glass plates with the development of celluloid film previously described.

Celluloid, a plasticlike material, was first developed in Europe during the 1860s and soon caught the attention of the photographic industry. One train of development experimented with slicing ultrathin sheets of this material, coating it with the usual photosensitive emulsion, and substituting these sheets for the heavier, breakable glass plate then in use. Another train of development led to a solution of nitrocellulose that could be poured and dried into a much thinner film. Eastman and his technical staff pursued this second course, eventually developing and patenting a process for producing and packaging long photosensitive strips of film in commercial quantities. Eastman declared celluloid film "the slickest product we have ever tried to make. The field for it is immense."[5] Even so, his initial attempt to market the new film was rebuffed by the professional photographers who then represented the bulk of the market. That early film produced images inferior to those of the established dry-plate technology. However, Eastman recognized how he could use this innovation to open up a huge new market among amateur photographers. An inexpensive handheld camera called the "Kodak" was designed to use the new roll film and was introduced into the market in 1888. It was just one part of an entire system for taking pictures, a system so simple that anyone could use it. For $25 the customer could purchase a Kodak loaded with a 100-

frame roll of film. Guided by a three-step process—
"pull the cord, turn the key, and press the button"—
the budding photographer could capture images of
life's ordinary moments and special passages. Once
the film roll was fully exposed, the customer simply
had to mail the camera and $10 to Eastman's plant in
Rochester, New York. There, the film would be
processed, the camera reloaded with fresh film, and
the prints and loaded camera mailed back to the customer.

"You press the button, we do the rest" became Eastman's advertising slogan throughout the world—a
proposition so appealing that the company had to
struggle for the next 10 years to satisfy demand. As
a success template–and fueled by developments in
motion-picture film, color film, photo-processing materials, and state-of-the-art manufacturing—it was
powerful enough to sustain almost a century of
growth and prosperity for the Eastman Kodak Company. By 1899, the company had purchased patents
and developed processes to switch from batch production of celluloid photo film to a process of continuous casting and coating. This made it possible to
dominate the market even as other firms fought des-
perately for a toe-hold.

Economies of scale made it possible to offer film
at low prices, further expanding the market. The company supplemented the initial U.S. and British distribution systems by agents worldwide, making
Eastman Kodak one of the world's early pioneers in
product globalization.

As shown in Figure 6.4, Eastman had now expanded its concept of value added to include the sim-
plification of the photographic process, providing low
prices to amateur and professional photographers.

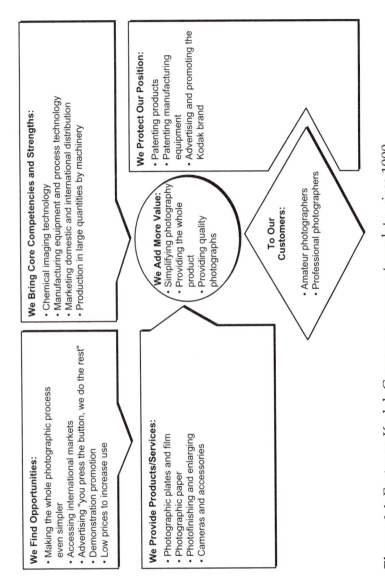

We Find Opportunities:

- Making the whole photographic process even simpler
- Accessing international markets
- Advertising "you press the button, we do the rest"
- Demonstration promotion
- Low prices to increase use

We Provide Products/Services:

- Photographic plates and film
- Photographic paper
- Photofinishing and enlarging
- Cameras and accessories

We Bring Core Competencies and Strengths:

- Chemical imaging technology
- Manufacturing equipment and process technology
- Marketing domestic and international distribution
- Production in large quantities by machinery

We Protect Our Position:

- Patenting products
- Patenting manufacturing equipment
- Advertising and promoting the Kodak brand

We Add More Value:

- Simplifying photography
- Providing the whole product
- Providing quality photographs

To Our Customers:

- Amateur photographers
- Professional photographers

Figure 6.4 Eastman Kodak Company success template, circa 1900.

It is interesting to contrast the success template shown in Figure 6.4 with those of other companies. For example, Microsoft was a latecomer in PC application software, including spreadsheets, word processing, and graphics. Yet its competitors, the firms that created those businesses, have fallen by the wayside or have been forced to reinvent themselves with new products. In these cases, being first to market was not nearly as important as having the right success template; in fact, George Eastman's success template of the late nineteenth century is not unrelated to the one that propels Microsoft's success today. Both sought to simplify their products and their use (from DOS to Windows), and both moved from professional to consumer markets.

Growth to Maturity

By 1902 photography was a huge business, and Eastman Kodak owned 80 to 90 percent of it.[6] The market would continue to grow worldwide for the next 70 years driven by demographics, consumer purchasing power, real cost reductions, and technological improvements. That growth continues in many international markets today. Eastman Kodak was not always the technical leader or first to market with new products, but it was quick to recognize opportunities and capitalize on them to achieve number-one market share. Its R&D capabilities made this possible. Over the entire period from 1900 through 1960, Kodak continued to improve the quality of every step of the photographic process, besting new competitors like Agfa, Gevert, and Fuji and maintaining market hegemony.

Even after an antitrust decision of the late 1950s forced the company to unbundle its film and film processing, opening the photo-processing market to independent producers, the power of the Eastman Kodak brand image—one of the world's strongest—allowed the company to continue its domination. Figure 6.5 shows the success template for the Eastman Kodak photography business in the period between 1960 and 1970. As indicated, Kodak added value with the best brand image in the marketplace, one that provided substantial consumer draw to the retailer. It provided the whole product and supported that product with intensive advertising. Even competing photo-processors would boast, "We use Kodak paper and chemicals." Sales of chemicals and supplies to other photo-processors were also very profitable.

Maturity and Beyond

The success template of Eastman Kodak positioned it to be an immensely profitable company as photography matured in the 1960s and 1970s. It was clearly number one, but the world was changing. By 1980, the company had reached the proverbial fork in the road that is part of phase 4 of the life-cycle model. It enjoyed one of the world's most-recognized brand names and had a distribution system that any global producer would envy; however, it had to either renew its core businesses or lose the premier position its founder had established a century earlier. The chemicals and materials-based technology on which George Eastman had built the company's global empire was over 100 years old and giving way to new imaging technology. Its ability to innovate product and manu-

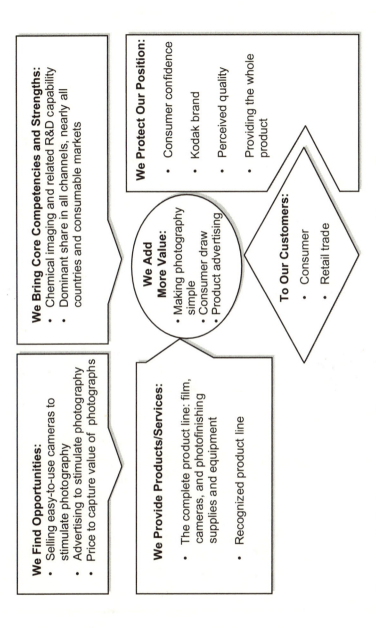

Figure 6.5 Eastman Kodak Company success template in the 1960s.

We Find Opportunities:
- Selling easy-to-use cameras to stimulate photography
- Advertising to stimulate photography
- Price to capture value of photographs

We Bring Core Competencies and Strengths:
- Chemical imaging and related R&D capability
- Dominant share in all channels, nearly all countries and consumable markets

We Add More Value:
- Making photography simple
- Consumer draw
- Product advertising

We Protect Our Position:
- Consumer confidence
- Kodak brand
- Perceived quality
- Providing the whole product

We Provide Products/Services:
- The complete product line: film, cameras, and photofinishing supplies and equipment
- Recognized product line

To Our Customers:
- Consumer
- Retail trade

facturing processes appropriate for the next wave of imaging technology would determine whether this great company either enjoyed a renaissance or a long period of decline.

By 1980 Kodak had become a complex portfolio company, with business units serving amateur and professional photographers with film, photo-processing materials, photo equipment, medical imaging, copiers, instant photography, and prepress. It had even acquired Sterling Drug, a pharmaceutical concern. The heart of this portfolio and the major source of its profits, however, was the film business, and so it was to remain. Neither the commercial copier nor the electronic prepress businesses enjoyed long-term success. At the same time, a disastrous experience with the Kodak disc camera marked a lapse of attention to the company's camera products. Eventually, the company sold off the copiers and Sterling. Instant photography embroiled the company in a costly patent dispute with Polaroid and had to be discontinued. By the early 1990s, the company's portfolio was in tatters and its profitability continued to hinge on the color-film business.

By now, even Eastman Kodak's core business was threatened. Imaging technology was poised in the midst of another transition—this time from chemically coated film to digital forms. One of the first manifestations of that transition occurred in amateur motion-picture photography, where Eastman Kodak's business was totally eclipsed by videotape and the now ubiquitous video camera. This proved to be a harbinger of things to come in Kodak's core business—doubly so, because many consumers bypassed still photography entirely in favor of video. By the mid-1990s, digital cameras began to surface and enter the market. These had the potential to do to film photography what the video camera had done to Kodak's home-movie business.

Digital cameras do not use film; instead, they create images on electronic memory cards that can be viewed, enhanced, edited, and printed via personal computers. This new approach to imaging presents a major threat because the entire product cycle of film, photographic paper, and development chemicals can be eliminated. Also, the competencies required in the world of digital imaging—electronics and computer science—are outside Kodak's success template, which is based on chemicals, process technology, and non-equipment consumables.

Kodak's success template based on consumable film is very different from the one used by the consumer electronics companies that it has begun to face in the new digital world. There, speed and flexibility are key; Sony and other electronics firms like it have succeeded by continually developing innovative new equipment and related manufacturing processes. Meanwhile, Kodak has been pouring some $500 million a year into digital-imaging R&D, but the payoff has been unclear. In 1997 its digital business lost some $200 million.[7] The company is finding it difficult to focus on both film and the digital world at the same time.

Figure 6.6 demonstrates the gap between these two templates. The question for Kodak and its management is, can Kodak negotiate this gap?

As a result of accumulating failures, Kodak was forced to contract as it moved into the 1990s, actively reducing costs to remain profitable. This may have been the right strategy given the circumstances, but it would do nothing to renew the fortunes of the company. As Dwight Gertz once warned downsizers in

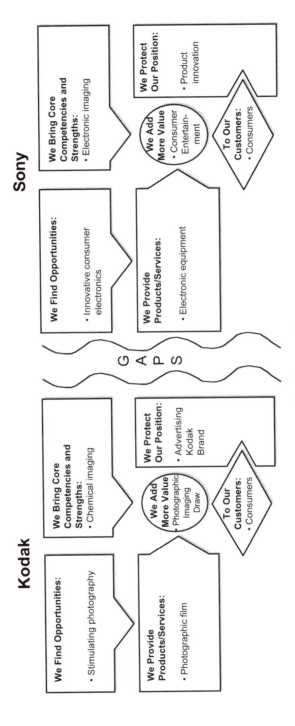

Figure 6.6 Two different success templates: Kodak and Sony.

general, "You cannot shrink to greatness." However, a company can continue to shrink to preserve profitability. The market for images that record the lives of families worldwide will always exist and will grow as the world's population increases. But the jury is out as to which company will dominate that market.

THE CHALLENGE OF BUSINESS LIFE CYCLES

Business life cycles present serious challenges to the portfolio manager, and many forget two important things: (1) that each portfolio unit has it own success template and (2) that the portfolio units are seldom at the same phase of the life cycle. Thus, unit A may be in the expansion phase, without large profits but successfully converting customers and gaining market share with a unique and proprietary product. Unit B, in contrast, may be at the phase 4 fork in the road, making profits hand over fist but facing a bleak future unless it re-creates itself with a winning new success template.

Numbers-driven senior managers who fail to appreciate the differences between these two units and where they stand in the life cycle may shut down unit A—their best hope for the future—while continuing to sink resources in unit B. "Unit B is producing a very high ROI," they may tell themselves, "so let's direct our resources there. Unit A is a leader in its field, but it provides no significant profits for us." That is precisely the type of thinking that drove the early conglomerate companies into the ground and that continues today in many portfolio companies. A short-term-profit orientation also discourages the search for alternatives to the current business and the business R&D needed to find the next success template (i.e., "If it isn't broken, don't fix it").

Another challenge in portfolio management is finding senior managers who are sufficiently broad in their thinking to provide oversight and encouragement to portfolio units. A manager advanced to the senior corporate ranks because of his or her success in a mature division driven by low-cost production may lack patience with units at the early tinkering phase of business R&D. Most corporations, in fact, focus on the management style appropriate for established businesses. Consider the Baby Bells in the late 1980s. They purchased or founded paging, computer-retailing, software, and publishing companies. Unlike their mature parent companies, each of these businesses sought a success template based on the convergence of information and telecommunications technologies. There were more business R&D experiments here than in normal operating companies. Nevertheless, the Baby Bell's tried to run them like established local telephone companies, with uniformly bad results.

The focus of business R&D should be on finding potentially successful templates for capturing markets and eliminating those likely to fail. Once a new success template has been found, senior management should give unit managers the resources and encouragement needed to drive toward a commanding market share. Too many companies, like Litton Industries mentioned previously, created the initial product that launches a whole new business only to fall by the wayside. Smith Kline & French, for example, created the anti-ulcer drug Tagemet and enjoyed a great deal of success. Greater energy on the part of Glaxo, however, succeeded in making its near-equivalent drug,

Zantac, the best-selling pharmaceutical of the 1980s. Superior marketing and product positioning by Glaxo helped it to eclipse its rival, even though it was second to market with a basically similar product.

During the expanding phase of the business life cycle, corporate management should focus on and encourage a management style that wins market share and builds positions of competitive advantage. Profits are important, but they are definitely secondary to building market dominance.

Once the business enters the established phase, profitability and protection of market position should be the dominant management concerns. This is also the time to begin looking for a new success template—one capable of renewing the business and blunting the natural tendency to enter a period of contraction. Finding the new success template is a lot more complicated than the 1970s approach of sorting the portfolio by cash cows, stars, dogs, and question marks. It is also a lot more rewarding.

7

Value Management in the Capital-Intensive Portfolio

Chapter 3 demonstrated how shareholder value is built through proper allocation of expenses across a portfolio of businesses. But, what about capital? What is the difference between capital and expense when you allocate resources? Isn't it all cash in the end? Yes, it's all cash, but differences in accounting practices make a big difference in how shareholders view capital versus expense. This difference leads to the concept of the *capital efficient frontier,* which defines the trade-off between capital expenditures and shareholder value.

This chapter shows you how to define your own capital efficient frontier by using the dialogue process described in Chapter 2. This process is very different than those normally used in constructing capital budgets because its focus is on the development of creative value-building alternatives. This dialogue process leaves little room for advocacy by powerful executives, and it focuses the entire organization on its primary task—value creation. This chapter also explores value creation in cyclical capital-intensive businesses, and nearly all capital-intensive businesses are cyclical.

Previous chapters have demonstrated the difficult trade-offs faced by decision makers in expense-driven businesses—pharmaceutical firms, retailing companies, consumer packaged-goods companies and so on. In many cases, they must choose between strategies that maximize earnings on one extreme and greater shareholder value on the other. The rule book of the accounting profession is often the source of these difficult choices. Generally accepted accounting principles do not allow expenses to be capitalized—even when they are invested in projects that clearly build long-term shareholder wealth. Instead, they must be charged against current earnings. As a consequence, investments in R&D, brand building, and other activities whose results will be felt in the future sap the current bottom line, making business performance look less robust than perhaps it should. In most cases, these expenditures must be ongoing: The R&D pipeline must be filled on a regular basis, and brand equity must be fortified periodically with promotional outlays.

Capital-intensive companies face different trade-offs, again in part because of accounting rules. The expenditures they make to build shareholder value can be capitalized. This means that the most important efficient frontier for capital-intensive companies relates capital expenditures to shareholder value.

Because businesses that are capital intensive are allowed to amortize their investments in long-term wealth-creating projects, they can spread the negative financial impact of investments over many years—even offsetting them with revenues that eventually flow from those investments. These companies face similar pressures as other companies from Wall Street when reporting short-term earnings, but the short-term impact of their investments is much less. The result is that business leaders have the flexibility to do what's best for the company in the long run without being bad-mouthed by stock analysts if long-term investments make a few quarterly-earnings reports look bad. Executives can do the right thing without negatively impacting everybody's bonuses.

The ability to capitalize investments can soften the blow to the bottom line and relieve CEOs of the pressure of analysts and nervous shareholders. Stock analysts and shareholders are rarely able to judge the merits of long-term investments and so scrutinize them far less carefully than they do current earnings—which are simple and seemingly straightforward. Lacking the abundant information and analysis required to weigh an investment's merits, they are forced to trust (or distrust) the judgment of management and patiently await the outcome of their choices. The result is that major wrongheaded investments can slip by unchallenged, and years pass before their destructive consequences are observed and tallied.

In the world of capital-intensive commerce, little mistakes have large consequences, and it is very easy to trap mountains of cash in investments that do little to create long-term shareholder value. This was a lesson learned by anyone who worked around the steel industry during the late 1960s and 1970s. Big Steel in the United States invested hundreds of millions—if not billions—of dollars during that period in the upgrading of old plants. These behemoth facilities were already among the most highly capitalized in the world but were generally outmoded and absorbed multimillion dollar upgrades without a hiccup.

Anyone who drives along the southern shore of Lake Michigan and other traditional U.S. steelmaking centers can see at a glance the result of those megainvestments: acres of industrial wasteland, idle plants surrounded by empty parking lots, and weed-infested landscapes where the most powerful engines of U.S. industry once stood. The millions invested in these locations are now gone and will never be recovered.

Ironically, at the very time that the United States' big steel producers were making these megablunders, other smaller companies were directing capital into new and unconventional approaches to steelmaking. They were recycling scrap steel and utilizing new minimill technology to make basic steel products. Nucor, then a small player, was only a few years away from constructing a new plant based on an unproven German technology for continuous casting of sheet steel, the holy grail of generations of steelmakers.[1] These minimills started making very simple steel products, such as reinforcing bars. From that base, they moved into more sophisticated products, such as steel joists and, eventually, coiled steel for the automobile industry. By degrees the minimill operators moved up the product chain, taking business away from Big Steel *and* the best of the foreign producers. They were creating a new success template within the heart of a mature industry that pundits had declared to be hopelessly in decline in North America.

The established U.S. steelmakers did not knowingly pour their financial assets down dry holes. On the contrary, they invested in projects that economic analysis indicated would pay off in terms of standard measures: pay out, ROI, or NPV. These investments, however, were viewed in isolation—that is, the big steel companies viewed a positive NPV for any particular project as creating value for the corporation as a whole. Following this logic, investments were pursued in piecemeal fashion: a basic oxygen furnace installed here, new materials transferring equipment and new milling lines installed there. They did not consider strategic alternatives. These plant improvements had the same effect as would upgrading the electronics aboard a cargo ship whose leaky hull was rusting away. A sound investment in one part of an obsolete mill will never make the entire plant competitive in an increasingly competitive world.

In hindsight it is fairly clear that the big steelmakers should have taken a strategic perspective instead of a project perspective to their investments. They should have asked, "What set of actions—taken together—will allow us to make and deliver the best steel at the lowest cost?" The answer to this strategic question would have led them out of the industrial doldrums and onto a higher-level frontier of business choices.

The big steelmakers were not the only companies to lock up massive amounts of capital in unrewarding projects. General Motors did the same under the chairmanship of Roger Smith during the early 1980s when it invested billions in plant modernization in a failed effort to become competitive with the Japanese manufacturers on the basis of cost and quality.[2] General Motors' major problem in the 1980s was its product line, which failed to excite many U.S. drivers. Investing in automation to make these products at lower costs did little to increase their appeal. The Japanese had already proven that capital was but one component in the twin tasks of improving quality and reducing costs. Despite massive capital spending on plant automation, GM's market share dropped almost 15 percent and the company continued to experience a cost disadvantage in its North American operations. Poor execution of the plant-modernization projects merely compounded the problem.

Meanwhile, across town, GM's smaller domestic rivals were also making capital investments in the 1980s, but theirs were smaller and more strategically targeted. Ford restructured its plants and invested heavily in new models—the highly successful Taurus and Explorer models being notable examples. For its part, Chrysler focused on product development and the engineering processes for speeding products to market. Although the investments made by Ford and Chrysler were small compared to GM's multibillion dollar venture, these companies *gained* market share, and both are today more productive and more profitable than their larger rival.

Smith's error at GM was in failing to see that competing in the changing North American automobile market required more than factory automation. Design innovation, product, time to market, and customer-perceived quality were equally important. But as strategic alternatives, these failed to draw serious funding at GM. Current GM management, which is clearly more strategic in its outlook, surely must wish that it had Roger Smith's billions to deploy today. Unfortunately, that money is gone forever.

FINDING THE CAPITAL EFFICIENT FRONTIER

In the first case, the steel industry, investments were made piecemeal without clear strategic intent. In the second case, at GM, one strategy was royally funded with no apparent seeking of better alternatives. The outcome in both instances was that these companies operated below the level of value creation that their immense capital and human talents should have made possible. In effect, they were classic economic underachievers, operating far below the efficient frontier of opportunities that their rivals managed to find and achieve.

These companies and others can find their efficient frontiers through the dialogue process described in Chapters 2 and 3. That process, revisited in Figure 7.1, is the same for capital-intensive and expense-driven

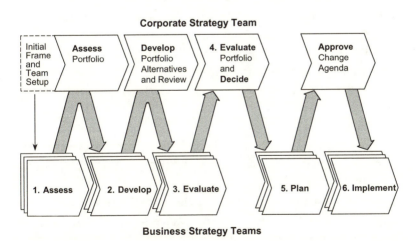

Figure 7.1 The dialogue process.

companies. In this process, step 1, assessment, motivates the search for alternatives; step 2 develops value-enhancing alternative strategies for each business unit; and step 3 evaluates the risk and return of these alternatives. The other steps in the process are deciding to move forward, developing an action plan, and implementing the plan.

To illustrate the application of this process for a capital-intensive business, the following discussion uses the example of a real company disguised through the numbers and context.

ChemTek

The example company, "ChemTek," produces the raw materials required for its manufactured chemicals and makes a primary chemical, polymers, and related products 1 and 2. In addition, it has an attractive new-product opportunity, one that will require a major investment in new plants and has the potential to become a new business unit. ChemTek's raw-materials business serves its primary-chemical business unit. The primary-chemical unit, in turn, serves each of the downstream business units, including polymers, product 1, product 2, and potentially, the new-product business.

The industry in which ChemTek participates is highly cyclical, and the price of the primary chemical fluctuates widely with the phases of the cycle. Both the raw materials and manufactured chemicals also experience substantial short-term swings in supply and demand, part of which can be explained by the behavior of participating companies. At the top of the cycle, these companies typically add capacity. When the crunch comes, the market is awash in excess capacity and the less-efficient participants take major losses.

The following shows how ChemTek can use the dialogue process to find its efficient frontier.

Step 1: Business Assessment

Any assessment of the business must begin with a quantification of the NPV or each of the current portfolio units and any anticipated projects. The NPV should not be represented as a single number but as a *range* of possible outcomes under various scenarios. Figure 7.2 presents this analysis for ChemTek's current strategy. Using the raw-materials unit as an example, there is only a 10 percent chance that its NPV will be less than $1,084 million and a 10 percent chance that it will exceed $3,498 million. The 50/50

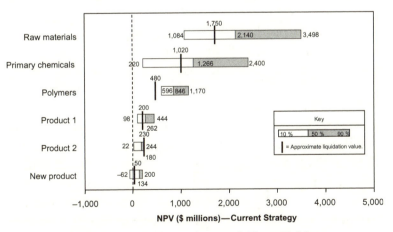

Figure 7.2 Value and risk analysis of ChemTek's current strategy.

value is $2,140 million. The 50/50 value represents the value at which there is an equal probability that the actual outcome will be higher or lower.

Finally, ChemTek would realize $1,750 million after taxes if it sold its raw-materials business. Using the 50/50 value of $2,140 million minus the after-tax liquidation value of $1,750 million, management is adding $390 million by retaining the business in its portfolio under the current strategy. (Here, the liquidation value is fairly certain.) Of course, the company hopes to add even more value when it looks at alternatives to the current raw-materials strategy.

Periodically examining the liquidation value of businesses in the portfolio is an essential part of effective portfolio management. (Of course, it is essential that the values of retaining or selling a business be computed accurately on an after-tax basis using the correct cost of capital. Even when potential buyers are willing to pay high premiums, effective management adds value on an after-tax basis.) If management is not adding value to the businesses in its portfolio over and above their after-tax liquidation values, those businesses should not be in the portfolio.

Assessment indicates that, by retaining most of the business units in the portfolio, management is adding considerable value over the potential liquidation value utilizing the 50/50 scenario. The exception is product 2; there, the 50/50 value is $180 million, but the liquidation value is approximately $230 million. This raises a red flag. Is the company better off selling this business or finding a higher value-creating alternative? The new-product business represents another red flag. In this case, there is approximately a 40 percent probability that the shareholder value of the business will be negative and a 10 percent chance that it will be worth a *negative* $62 million or less versus its potential after-tax liquidation value of $50 million. At the same time, the 50/50 value is $134 million. The challenge for ChemTek is to find strategies that will mitigate the downside risks of the new-product business and enhance its upside value.

Business assessment must also provide a view of the corporation as a whole, including risk. What are the risks associated with the overall portfolio of the business? Figure 7.2 indicates the risks associated with the individual businesses, but the risk of the overall portfolio is bound to differ. Each of ChemTek's units is sensitive to the price of the primary chemical. A big price change would naturally affect all units.

As with just about everything else, the price of the primary chemical has experienced a real-dollar downtrend. That downtrend has generally benefited the downstream units because they have had to pay less for an input to their own products. Despite this real-dollar downtrend, there have been substantial fluctuations in the price of ChemTek's primary chemical over the past 30 years. Like most capital-intensive commodities—from aluminum to memory chips—the primary-chemical price fluctuates substantially over its business cycle. The last section of the present chapter will explore further this cyclical nature. In addition to the fluctuations, cycles of the industry have been very unpredictable. These uncertainties with respect to the primary chemical are illustrated in Figure 7.3, a sensitivity analysis aimed at showing the impact of a change in price on the value of different portfolio businesses. This figure indicates a $4.8 billion value for the ChemTek Corporation. The raw-materials and primary-chemicals units prosper when the primary-chemical price is high. The shareholder value of the

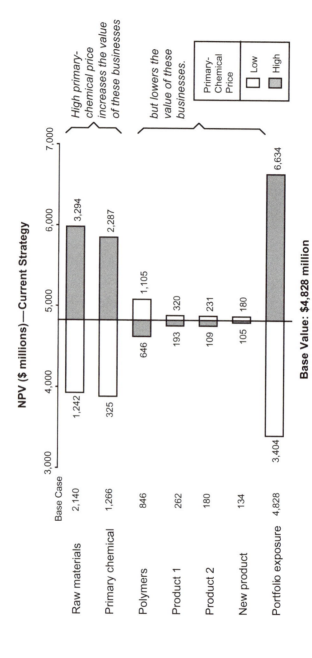

Figure 7.3 Risk for ChemTek due to price of the primary chemical.

downstream businesses on the other hand (polymers, product 1, product 2, and the new product) all react negatively to high primary-chemical price because they must use this chemical as an input but are not always able to pass along input costs to their customers. Although there is a 50/50 chance that the shareholder value of ChemTek is $4.8 billion, there is a 10 percent probability that it will be less than $3.4 billion and a 10 percent probability that it could be higher than $6.6 billion.

The analysis just described indicates that the company faces a challenge in achieving a better balance between the upstream and downstream portions of its business. Complete risk balancing would put Chem-Tek in a zero-risk position with respect to the price of the primary chemical—the upstream exposure would be completely offset by the downstream price exposure. Chapter 8 returns to this challenge.

Ideally, a company would want the bar representing portfolio exposure in Figure 7.3 to be as narrow as possible. As this figure indicates, the downstream businesses suffer when the prices of raw materials and the primary chemical rise because they must use these materials in their products. This underscores the fact that the different portfolio units—and their various strategies—are *not* independent. This lack of independence represents a challenge to the company's strategic alternatives, something addressed in Chapter 8.

At this point, readers versed in integrated capital-intensive businesses may be highly skeptical. "We tried to balance upstream and downstream risk, and it was a disaster," they may say. This, in fact, is what happened in the aluminum industry; the reason was that the downstream businesses (e.g., aluminum cans, automotive parts, construction material, etc.) focused on moving tonnage instead of profitability. Rather than letting the upstream businesses take the hit when aluminum prices were low, senior executives have typically tried to make up for low prices with more production. In a cyclic industry, this strategy is a disaster because it drives down prices further.

It is a paradox that risk balancing can only be achieved when every business unit is forced to act as a profit center, paying the market price for its inputs and selling its outputs at the market price. In the aluminum and other industries, there is a definite advantage to having balance between the up- and downstream portions of the business, provided that the downstream sells value-added products priced to value and not priced to the tons of aluminum in the product. In fact, competition and customer power can make risk balancing difficult if the products are not value added. If products are not value added, customers will insist on capturing the value of low primary-material prices. Aluminum cans are a classic example. Bottlers such as Coca-Cola demand that low aluminum prices be passed through to them; but when aluminum prices were high, they refuse to accept pass-through of those higher prices. Risk balancing works well, however, when the product is high value added, such as proprietary aluminum parts and components sold to the auto industry.

Step 2: Develop Alternative Strategies

As discussed in previous chapters, the development of alternative strategies requires the identification of potentially attractive initiatives. In a capital-intensive company, these initiatives generally take the form of capital projects for new plants, debottlenecking operations, process improvements, and so on. However, other types of initiatives can be even more valuable and are often overlooked: new-product development, marketing, development of new distribution capabilities, and new supplier and customer relationships. Growth in shareholder value in most cases is based on the successful pursuit of multiple initiatives. Figure 7.4 shows how multiple initiatives in just one portfolio unit (raw materials) can be screened to determine the best initiative. In this figure, the competing initiatives for the raw-materials business are arrayed in terms of capital productivity (NPV created per NPV of capital expended) in descending order of productivity from left to right. Of those shown, only the new greenfield site facility *reduces* shareholder value. All other proposed initiatives will earn more than their

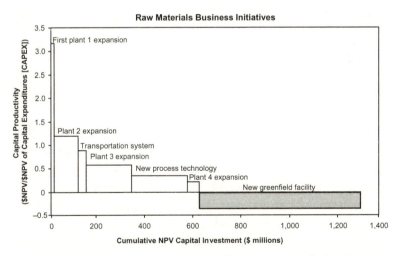

Figure 7.4 Capital productivity of raw-materials business initiatives.

cost of capital. However, as discussed in the next section, that doesn't mean that corporate management should accept every initiative that has a positive payoff. Instead, the business unit should combine its initiatives into alternative strategies that have a common purpose and result in higher value added.

Strategic Portfolio Alternatives for ChemTek

From the example of one portfolio unit, the discussion can move to the portfolio as a whole. Table 7.1 shows a strategy table indicating the range of alternative strategies for each of the six businesses in ChemTek's portfolio. For example, the primary-chemical business has determined its alternatives to be the following:

- Sell assets.
- Maintain existing facilities at full capacity.
- Invest in the plant 1 and plant 2 expansions, plus develop a new transportation system to access new markets and to reduce costs.
- Expand all facilities, add new process technology and the new transportation system.

The options shown in Table 7.1 represent each unit's unique opportunities to create value for ChemTek. Each business unit has a full range of alternatives, ranging from monetizing its assets (as through a sale of assets) through various approaches to growth: maintain, moderate, and aggressive. The question is, "Which combination of unit alternatives will create the greatest benefit for the company's shareholders?"

Table 7.1 Alternative portfolio strategies for ChemTek.

	Business-Unit Strategies					
Portfolio Strategy	Raw Materials	Primary Chemicals	Polymers	Product 1	Product 2	New Product
Monetize	Sell assets	Sell assets	Sell business	Sell business	Sell business	Sell technology
Maintain/harvest	Maintain full capacity, defer expansions	Maintain existing facilities at minimal levels for safe operation	Maintain existing market volumes	Maintain existing plants	Focus on current postprofitable customers	Not applicable
Moderate growth	Plant 1 and plant 2 expansions, plus new transportation system	Bring existing facilities to full production levels	Debottleneck current facility, improve product quality	Add new plants and grow market share	Develop enhanced products to maintain current market position	Go slow on commercialization until R&D demonstration
Aggressive growth	Expand all facilities, plus new technology and transportation	Expand existing facilities	Expand into Asia	Add new products, grow market share, and enter automotive market	Enhanced products and major Latin American initiative	Develop international joint venture strategy in parallel with product development

Step 3: Evaluate the Portfolio Alternatives

To select the best portfolio strategy for ChemTek, the first job is to evaluate the alternative strategies shown in Table 7.1 and determine the shareholder value created, earnings, and risk for each. Figure 7.5 begins this process by showing the calculated shareholder value and risk for each alternative. The figure illustrates that the aggressive strategies add significant value to the portfolio, with the exception of the product 2 business, which should be considered for sale. The alternatives in the downstream businesses add substantial value with the exception of product 2 and will result in a better-balanced company. However, upstream and downstream risks will not be balanced in total (see Figure 7.3).

The final task of this evaluation is to render these many strategic alternatives into a set of trade-offs between capital expenditures and the expected shareholder value in order to identify ChemTek's efficient frontier. This is shown in Figure 7.6. Points on the efficient frontier represent the best trade-offs between shareholder value and capital expenditures, in this case, NPV of capital to be expended per share. Each of these points represents the calculated outcome of a unique path across the strategy table shown in Table 7.1 (Note: If each possible path were represented, there would be 3,072 points on Figure 7.6—calculated as 4 to the 5th power times 3. Those not shown here fall below the efficient frontier.) The company's current strategy is also indicated in Figure 7.6. As you can see, it falls far beneath the company's efficient frontier.

To interpret the efficient frontier shown in this figure, start with strategy A located at the extreme lower

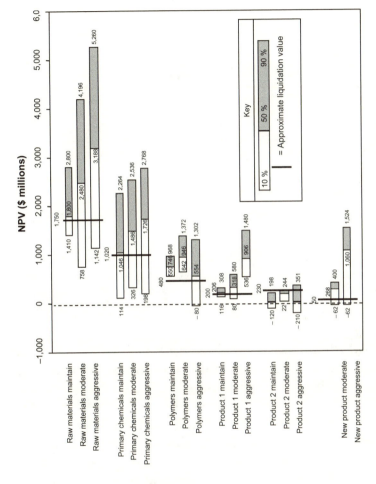

Figure 7.5 Risk analysis of ChemTek business-unit alternatives.

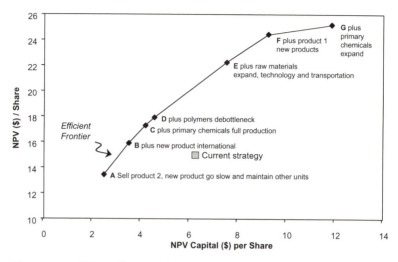

Figure 7.6 The efficient frontier for ChemTek.

end of the frontier. This strategy is a unique combination of portfolio-unit choices—a path through the
strategy table shown in Table 7.2. The light boxes represent what each Portfolio unit would do under this
strategy: The product 2 business is sold, the new product unit follows a go-slow approach, and all other
units maintain their current operations. As a whole,
this strategy has a value of about $13.40 per share and
requires a capital program of about $2.50 per share.

In contrast, strategy F, found near the opposite end
of the efficient frontier, is characterized by a very
different set of choices for the various portfolio units.
These are indicates by boxes outlined in bold in
Table 7.2. Here, product 2 will again be sold, but with
other alternatives that differ:

- The raw-materials unit will expand all of its facilities.

Table 7.2 Strategies A and F for ChemTek.*

	Business-Unit Strategies					
	Raw Materials	Primary Chemicals	Polymers	Product 1	Product 2	New Product
	Sell assets	Sell assets	Sell business	Sell business	Sell business	Sell technology
	Maintain full capacity, defer expansions	Maintain existing facilities at minimal levels for safe operation	Maintain existing market volumes	Maintain existing plants	Focus on current postprofitable customers	Not applicable
	First plant 1 and plant 2 expansions, plus new transportation system	Bring existing facilities to full production levels	Debottleneck current facility, improve product quality	Add new plants and grow market share	Develop enhanced products to maintain current market position	Go slow on commercialization until R&D demonstration
	Expand all facilities, plus new technology and transportation	Expand existing facilities	Expand into Asia	Add new products, grow market share, and enter automotive market	Enhanced products and major Latin American initiative	Develop international joint venture strategy in parallel with product development

*Choices for strategy A are unmarked; choices for strategy F are in boldlined boxes.

- Primary chemical will bring each of its facilities up to full capacity.
- Debottlenecking and quality initiatives will occupy the polymer unit.
- The product 1 group will add new products, grow the market share, and enter the automotive market.
- The new-product group will move forward with product development and a joint-venture strategy.

The more aggressive approach of strategy F would create a bit over $24 per share in value at a cost of slightly more than $9 of NPV capital per share.

Choices for Decision Makers

Of the over 3,000 strategic choices available through this type of methodology, ChemTek's executives need only consider those along the efficient frontier, shown in Figure 7.6.

A. Maintain the raw-materials, primary-chemicals, polymer-chemicals, and product 1 business units; sell the product 2 business and go slow on commercialization of the new product until the R&D demonstration is complete.

B. Same as A except that the new-product business strategy moves to aggressive development of an international joint venture in parallel with product development.

C. Same as B except that the primary-chemicals strategy turns to bringing existing facilities into full production.

   D. The same as C except that the polymers strategy
      becomes debottlenecking the current facility and
      improving product quality.
   E. Same as D except that the raw-materials strat-
      egy turns to expanding all facilities, plus invest-
      ing in new technology and transportation
      systems.
   F. Same as E except that the product 1 strategy
      changes to adding new products, growing mar-
      ket share, and entering the automotive market.
   G. Same as F except that the primary-chemicals
      strategy changes to expanding existing facilities.

The company's current strategy likewise can be tossed
in the wastebasket. The company also eliminated
strategy G, shown on the left-most end of the frontier,
because it adds very little value over the cost of capital
for the extra investment it requires. Eliminating these
reduces the decision-making chore to a manageable
size.

Because no single strategy on the frontier is inherently superior to any other, executives must debate
the trade-offs each represents. Ideally, all would want
the greater NPV produced by the right-most strategies
on the frontier, but the capital requirement of these
may strain ChemTek's financial capabilities. For one
reason or another, the company may not be able to obtain sufficient financing, or the financing itself may
change the company's capital structure to an undesir-
able extent.

This approach to making major strategic decisions
is very different than those normally found in capital-
intensive companies. Its objective methodology leaves
little or no room for advocacy by powerful executives;

this reduces a company's exposure to megamistakes such as the one committed by GM in the 1980s. It also requires that each business unit develop a manageable set of strategic alternatives to business as usual and that these be used to make decisions about how the business *as a whole* makes capital investments. The evaluation of the entire business strategy, instead of only individual projects, eliminates the chance that the corporation will pour millions into dead-end projects, as Big Steel did in earlier decades. The effect of every investment on the business as a whole is a key part of the decision process.

ALTERNATIVE STRATEGIES IN CYCLIC INDUSTRIES

This chapter began with a few observations about the differences between expense-driven and capital-intensive businesses. One of those differences is the extent to which they are roiled by business cycles. Food, drugs, packaged goods, and other expense-driven companies feel the ups and downs of economic cycles, but rarely to the extent that they impact capital-intensive companies. When the economy goes into recession, the people who make pretzels, Prozac, and motion pictures barely feel a ripple. Capital-intensive industries such as petroleum, chemicals, automobiles, machine tools, and semiconductors, on the other hand, experience jolting cycles of high and low demand. Expense-driven companies can often reduce their spending when customer demand contracts, but companies that sit atop billions-worth of factories and equipment must continue to meet their obligations even when they are plagued by periods of weak demand.

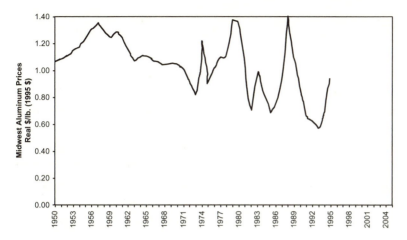

Figure 7.7 Aluminum industry price cycles.
Source: Navigant Consulting, Inc.

The cycles experienced by capital-intensive businesses are often very dramatic, as Figure 7.7 indicates for the aluminum industry. These price cycles are exacerbated by participants' own perverse tendencies to add capacity when new capacity is least needed. When customer sales are really humming, plants are running near full capacity, and customer orders are backing up, saying "yes" to any proposal to invest in new capacity is hard to resist, even though the downward phase of the industry cycle may be just around the corner. This pattern is so common that many economists no longer look at capital spending as a reliable leading indicator of economic growth.

To make matters worse, competitors are often making the same decision to add capacity at the same time; the result is a flood of new capacity coming online at the same time, often when the industry is heading into a slump. Ideally, new capacity should be timed to come onstream when demand is rising and approaching the point where current capacity cannot meet it. Unfortunately, no one's crystal ball is clear enough to accurately time this sort of decision.

In many cases, the best time to invest in new capacity is during the downward phase of the cycle. But this is when demand is falling, earnings are hemorrhaging, and gloom is pervasive. Adding capacity in this environment is about the last thing on anyone's mind.

The behavior that motivates this industrial version of buy high, sell low cannot be entirely explained by naïveté or hopeless optimism. Instead, five powerful forces bear on decisions that lead to overcapacity. The first is the need to satisfy customer demands, which often outstrips capacity as the peak of the business cycle approaches. Executives wisely recognize that they cannot fail to satisfy customer orders when reliability is the key to long-term customer-supplier relationships. Second, failing to invest during a cycle uptrend may leave the corporation awash in cash and make it a tempting target for a hostile raider. Third, executives fear that they will lose market share if they sit still while competitors are adding production capacity. Fourth, technology usually makes large new investments attractive because they reduce unit cost and provide other benefits, such as flexibility and reduced lead times. Finally, the uncertainty associated with capital-intensive cycles makes it difficult to know where one is in the cycle at any given time; what is clear in retrospect is largely guesswork at the moment a decision is called for.

To develop creative alternative strategies in cyclic industries, a company needs a thorough understanding of the dynamic supply-demand relationships of the industry during the business-assessment stage. This understanding must include (1) the uncertainties associated with both the amplitude and duration of future cycles and (2) the known or likely strategies of competitors (e.g., are they also planning new capacity?). Unfortunately, straight-line extrapolations of current data are a common feature of business analysis. In boom times, this leads to overprojection of future demand and the building of unneeded capacity.

At a minimum, a capital-intensive business needs to consider alternatives to *building* capacity. *Buying* capacity from struggling competitors is one of the most obvious of these alternatives. Production capacity can often be purchased at fire-sale discounts near the bottom of the cycle. In extreme cases, companies have sold plant and equipment at less than 10 cents on the dollar. Unfortunately, few companies have the means or the contrarian instincts to make major investments at these times even though careful analysis generally points to these periods as the best and least-risky times to invest.

Capacity expansion by whatever means should not be the only item on the list of alternatives for the capital-intensive company. In the steel and auto examples used to introduce this chapter, Chrysler, Ford, and Nucor operated in a world awash in capacity; their major gains were not scored through capacity expansions but from investment in even more powerful alternatives: process improvements, the introduction of new-product technology, and the development of new-product families.

This chapter explained how decision makers for capital-intensive companies can find their way to the efficient frontier, given their current business portfolios. The next chapter will show how to expand the efficient frontier by looking beyond the hand the company has been dealt and looking to acquisitions to meet corporate challenges.

8

Strengthening the Portfolio through Acquisitions

Acquisition can be an important tool for increasing shareholder value. In effect, an acquisition candidate represents another alternative to building value and a competitor to internal opportunities for selection and funding. Any acquisition can and should be evaluated using the methods described in previous chapters; the keys are knowing the corporation's efficient frontiers for its existing businesses and understanding the corporation's template for success. Only then can an acquisition be evaluated properly. Once a corporation has identified the efficient frontier of existing portfolio businesses, it can expand that frontier to see how potential acquisitions would fit in. Equally important, it can evaluate acquisitions proactively and respond quickly to hot deals that come its way.

Theoretically, the logic of increasing shareholder value through acquisition is simple and straightforward. The combined value of the acquiring company and the target company (or unit) should be greater than the value of the sum of the two separate entities. What could be simpler? Unfortunately, this is like saying that the way to make money in the stock market is to "buy low and sell high." Neither is easy.

THE CHECKERED HISTORY OF ACQUISITIONS

The public record on acquisitions is not encouraging. Most business acquisitions fail to meet the expectations of acquirers. Alexandra Reed Lajoux and J. Fred Weston have recently summarized what is known about mergers and acquisitions: "A compilation of studies shows mixed results on postmerger performance, depending on the criteria used to measure deals."[1] This is as true today as it was in the 1970s and 1980s. A *Business Week*–Mercer Management Consulting study of 150 major deals ($500 million plus) completed in the period from 1990 to 1995 found that only 17 percent created substantial returns for the acquiring companies, while 33 percent created marginal returns.[2] The other 50 percent actually *reduced* shareholder value (as measured by total return to shareholders relative to industry returns over a three-year period). Other studies indicate that 70 percent of acquisitions failed to meet the full expectations of the acquirer.

What explains this lackluster record? In general, three problems plague companies that seek growth through acquisitions:

1. *The greener-grass syndrome.* When executives view their current businesses as offering limited opportunities to create value, their first inclination is to look outside—even outside their industries—for growth. When they do, good stories are not hard to find. Unfortunately, executives who are intimately familiar with the success templates, problems, and risks associated with their current businesses are less able to see those associated with their acquisitions. The greener-grass syndrome results when executives and employees fail to rigorously seek alternatives within their own enterprises. It is always easier to believe, "We're not growing because we are in a lousy industry." Author consultant Dwight Gertz lists this tendency among his seven myths about business growth. Yes, some industries are afflicted with overcapacity, declining demand, and militant unions that make process improvement and restructuring difficult. Still, his research has identified high-growth companies in virtually *every* major industry, even in those that most readers would dismiss as stagnant.[3]

2. *Mismatches.* In many deals, there is little or no connection between the success templates that produced success for acquirer and acquired. The acquirer in these cases oftens tries to run both businesses with its own notion of what works—that is, its own success template. This is usually a recipe for disaster. For example, during the 1970s and 1980s, cash-rich oil companies went on an acquisition binge aimed at capturing strategic resources—coal, metals, and minerals. These, like oil, were all extraction businesses, but the similarities ended there. The oil business was not people-intensive; its headcount-to-sales ratio was very low compared to those of mining companies. The personnel and management policies that were

integral to success for the oil companies were a template for disaster when applied to copper and coal mining.

Some of the oil giants branched off into totally unrelated areas. Mobil bought the lethargic retail giant Montgomery Ward and, to no one's surprise, had no particular insights into reviving that company's flagging fortunes.

In other cases, acquirer and acquired found themselves at different points in the business life cycle with different success templates. So, when a mature giant like Exxon began dabbling with entrepreneurial office equipment and computer-electronics acquisitions, its success template was a mismatch with the success template in these high-growth businesses, which marched to a much different drum.

3. *Poor shopping methods.* Good shopping methods make it possible for acquirers to estimate the value and risks of a target. When decision makers lack the tools to find and evaluate internal opportunities, it is a safe bet that they will be even less equipped to evaluate the risks and returns of other companies or identify their options to increase value.

What is the value of the target business's current strategy to the acquirer's shareholders? Do the success templates fit together? What is the value of the target's strategic alternatives? In the absence of effective tools, acquirers must rely on less-than-objective methods, and their decisions are susceptible to overly optimistic projections. This problem is exacerbated when the company's advisers are highly incented to make a deal. Almost 20 years ago, Warren Buffett described the misplaced optimism of corporate acquirers in one of his widely read annual reports. His words could easily have been written yesterday: "Many managements apparently were over-exposed in impression-able childhood years to the story in which the impris-oned, handsome prince is released from the toad's body by a kiss from the beautiful princess. Conse-quently, they are certain that the managerial kiss will do wonders for the profitability of the target com-pany.... We've observed many kisses, but very few miracles. Nevertheless, many managerial princesses remain serenely confident about the future potency of the kisses, even after their corporate backyards are knee-deep in unresponsive toads."[4]

The poor record of most business acquisitions notwithstanding, a number of companies have made very successful acquisitions. General Motors is, in fact, the outcome of a series of successful acquisitions. So, too, is Citigroup. And although the returns are not yet in, Alcoa is consolidating the aluminum industry through acquisitions. In the high-tech arena, Cisco Sys-tems has an active and effective acquisition strategy. Cisco Systems uses acquisitions to obtain complemen-tary businesses and technologies. These acquisitions are an essential part of the company's success template, providing growth and access to new technologies and new markets. They are also in related businesses that have similar success templates, including marketing, manufacturing, and product-development competen-cies. These acquisitions diversify Cisco's technological risk while providing access to competing technologies.

Generally, an acquisition has a good opportunity to increase shareholder value if the following three con-ditions are satisfied:

1. *The acquisition increases shareholder value by im-proving the corporate efficient frontier.* This assumes, of

course, that the acquiring company has diligently sought internal alternatives and that it has subjected them *and* the acquisition opportunity to detailed and objective evaluation. By doing so, one can determine where an acquisition stands relative to a company's efficient frontier, thus providing a sure antidote to the greener-grass syndrome. Best of all, the internal efficient frontier can be determined before the need to evaluate a deal presents itself. Understanding this frontier simplifies the evaluation and can be used proactively to screen acquisition candidates.

Unfortunately, experience has repeatedly shown that most companies simply fail to seek out the value-generating alternatives that exist under their own roofs.

2. *The acquisition provides a good match with the corporation's success template or is part of a conscious effort to improve that template.* One could observe this principle in practice during the 1980s when a number of companies with proven templates for profitability used acquisitions to extend their operations geographically. Gannett (newspapers), Waste Management (trash), and Valspar (paints) all conducted ambitious campaigns to purchase small regional companies that could be operated more efficiently and profitably using their proven success templates. Greater scale and scope, together with operational efficiencies, made these strategies successful. The principle of finding and acquiring companies that can be operated well with a success template *that management understands* may be the best defense against the mismatch problem cited earlier. Alternatively, the acquiring corporation can commit to learning the success template of the acquired company and managing it according to that template. This is hard to do, and

even harder to pass on to succeeding management teams.

3. *The real value of the acquisition is clearly defined and its risks are both understood and manageable.* As described previously, the failure to define value and measure risks explains why so many companies do such a poor job in shopping for acquisitions. The antidote is for decision makers to employ rigorous and uncompromising methods of analysis—the kind described in previous chapters.

ACQUISITIONS MUST IMPROVE THE EFFICIENT FRONTIER

Imagine for a moment that you are the CEO of ChemTek, the company showcased in Chapter 7. Imagine further that your managers and staff people have neither identified nor evaluated the range of internal opportunities described in that chapter. None of these, in fact, have found their way onto your company's radar. Then imagine that you are meeting with an investment banker who is playing matchmaker for one of his client companies.

"Southwest Chemical would be an excellent acquisition for you," the banker intones with absolute confidence. "It's a solid company with lots of technical know-how, plant resources, and distribution. As a unit of ChemTek, it would do two very important things for your business: First, it would diversify away some of your current risks; second, it would provide balance between your upstream raw-materials business and your downstream value-adding product units. These make it a great fit for ChemTek and an excellent opportunity for growth."

Sounds good, you think to yourself as the banker continues. "The board of Southwest has the highest respect for you and your company, and I can assure you that we can arrange a deal on a very friendly and favorable basis—a win-win deal for both companies and their shareholders."

All of the banker's points seem to add up. You've already seen the numbers and consulted with your people, and all agree that the acquisition would be good for ChemTek. The chief financial officer's support for the deal is unqualified. As she said in her memo just the day before:

> Even at the premium price they're asking, the deal will pay for itself, including the cost of capital. We will show increased earnings the first year.

Your vice president of operations' assessment is equally upbeat:

> Southwest has low-cost primary-chemical production, outstanding polymer production plants, and large, profitable downstream businesses. Integration of our U.S. operations with theirs would give us substantial cost-reduction opportunities and establish us as the second-largest player in the downstream business.

The banker continues pressing his point. "Your business, like mine," he says earnestly, "is changing fast. Both are becoming dangerous games for small players. We must grow or die. Frankly, I suspect that's the reason that Southwest's chairman is willing to sell. This creates a growth opportunity for you, and all that it takes to capture it is a stroke of the pen. No muss, no fuss. No plants to build. No managers to hire. No distribution networks to build. And no hostile tenders to fight. The chips are on the table—all that you have to do is pick them up."

On the surface, the banker's proposal sounds like an important growth opportunity, and if you had found no internal alternatives for ChemTek's growth, you'd be duty bound to snap up Southwest, assuming that the price was right. Many executives, thousands in fact, find themselves in similar decision situations every year—and many follow the banker's advice and pull out their checkbooks. But would this acquisition represent a good decision by ChemTek?

The first step in evaluating an acquisition is to understand where it fits relative to current strategy and other opportunities. One can accomplish this by using the evaluation techniques described in previous chapters. The acquisition target is evaluated in the same way as internally generated alternatives, the goal being to determine where the acquisition falls relative to the company's efficient frontier. If it falls beneath the current efficient frontier, the acquisition opportunity will only diminish shareholder value and should be rejected. If it falls on or outside the current efficient frontier, the acquisition should be seriously considered.

Unfortunately, companies that fail to actively seek out internal alternatives and that lack the analytical know-how to evaluate the risks and returns of their strategic choices cannot determine their efficient frontiers or where their acquisition prospects stand relative to them. They must, instead, fall back on traditional methods of acquisition analysis.

To see how an acquisition can improve the efficient frontier, let's revisit the ChemTek case from Chapter 7. This company had made a systematic search for value-creating portfolio strategies within its existing operating units. Of the more than 3,000 internal portfolio alternatives found, recall that seven defined the best available trade-offs between invested capital and share value (Figure 8.1). The most promising of these to company decision makers—given their goals and resources—was portfolio alternative F; this required a capital investment of approximately $9 per share but was projected to be worth about $24 per share.

Remember that none of ChemTek's alternatives involves a single activity but represents a number of initiatives affecting the business portfolio. For example, strategy A would require ChemTek executives to do a number of things:

- Maintain the raw-materials business, primary-chemicals, polymer-chemicals, and product 1 business units.
- Sell the product 2 business.

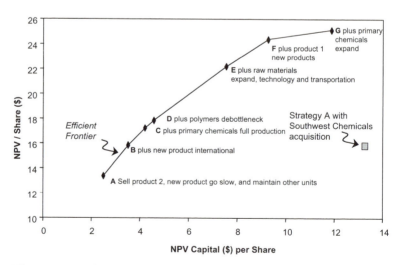

Figure 8.1 ChemTek's efficient frontier.

- Go slow on commercialization of the new product until the R&D demonstration is complete.

Having found the efficient frontier of internal alternatives, ChemTek has a baseline against which to judge the merits of potential acquisitions. At this point, the people at ChemTek ask, "Where would a Southwest Chemical acquisition fall relative to these other choices?" It seemed like a good choice earlier, before alternative portfolio strategies A through G were generated and quantified. When the analysis is done, however, the ChemTek people find that it falls well *below* the efficient frontier as shown in Figure 8.1. The acquisition is not bad in the sense that it would reduce shareholder value and company earnings; however, it is inferior to other, internal alternatives. The acquisition, then, is a poor alternative for ChemTek. An examination of the productivity of capital illustrates why this is true.

In reality, ChemTek was considering two other acquisitions:

- *A joint venture in Eastern Europe (EE-JV).* In this venture, ChemTek would acquire a 50 percent interest in and become the operator of a primary-chemicals plant. ChemTek would provide investment capital, technical expertise, and operating capabilities with the expectation of doubling production while dramatically reducing unit costs. In addition, ChemTek would gain access to markets currently suffering from a supply shortfall; these markets are expected to grow by 15 percent each year for at least the next 10 years.
- *Pacific Company (Pacific).* This acquisition would give ChemTek two new plants: one that produces

raw materials and another that produces the primary chemical. The first could be expanded to
twice its current capacity; the second's capacity
could be increased by an estimated 30 percent.
ChemTek engineers believe that production costs
at these plants can be significantly reduced,
whether or not their capacities are increased. Acquisition of Pacific would also give its new
owner greater opportunities for exports to Asia
and Australia.

Preliminary screening analysis indicates that each
of these, like Southwest Chemical (SW), has the potential to increase the ChemTek's earnings per share,
even after the cost of financing (through stock, debt,
or cash). But will these acquisitions fall above or below ChemTek's current efficient frontier?

Capital Productivity

The question that ChemTek's CEO needs to ask is,
"What is the productivity of the investment in the
Southwest Chemical acquisition?" A convenient way
to answer this question is to graph the ratio of the
change in NPV to the change in capital investment for
each internal and external alternative. This indicates
the productivity of each dollar of capital investment
for each alternative—that is, the bang for the buck.
(The same can be done for expense investments in
expense-driven businesses.) This is shown in Figure 8.2. For example, for portfolio strategy A, an investment of some $800 million, the capital productivity
of that capital is about 5.3, which means that the NPV
is $4.3 billion ($800 million multiplied by 5.3). (The
NPV of $4.3 billion includes the investment of $800

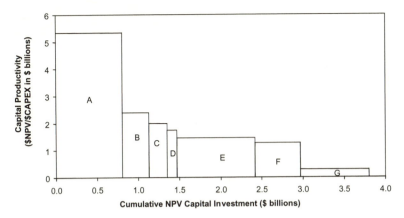

Figure 8.2 ChemTek's capital productivity without acquisitions.

million.) By determining the ratio for each alternative in this way and graphing them, it is easier to visualize the components of the efficient frontier. One can see at a glance the productivity of each potential capital investment and where each alternative strategy fits in. ChemTek would naturally invest in portfolio strategy A first because it clearly has the highest productivity of capital. Portfolio strategy B has the next-highest productivity of invested capital, and so forth.

Where do the acquisitions fit into ChemTek's capital productivity? To answer this question, ChemTek's CEO has his staff develop the NPV and productivity of the acquisitions utilizing the methods applied in Chapter 7. This makes it possible to see where the three acquisitions fit in the pecking order of capital productivity, as shown in Figure 8.3. (In the case of acquisitions, capital expenditure is the acquisition cost plus future capital contributions.) Figure 8.3 shows the CEO that EE-JV is potentially very attractive; its capital productivity is better than almost all internal possibilities. The Pacific acquisition is reasonably at-

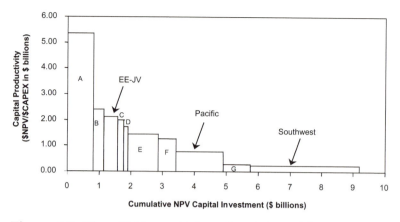

Figure 8.3 ChemTek's capital productivity with acquisitions.

tractive; however, most of the internal alternatives on the efficient frontier are even more attractive. The Southwest Chemical acquisition, not surprisingly, is a relatively unproductive investment, a poor use of the required $3.5 billion in capital.

By examining Figure 8.3, the CEO can see that if he has only so much capital available for investment, he should start at the left-hand side and move toward the right—that is, invest first in strategy A because it provides the greatest level of capital productivity. If he has more capital to invest, he should move on to strategy B, then to the acquisition EE-JV, and so forth. This is analogous to the capital-budgeting prioritizing method with which many business executives are familiar. However, in this case, any decision to acquire EE-JV or another external opportunity must consider the match with ChemTek's success template and the company's ability to define and manage the risks.

Once the analysis is complete, one can graph the results in terms of the efficient frontier, as shown in Fig-

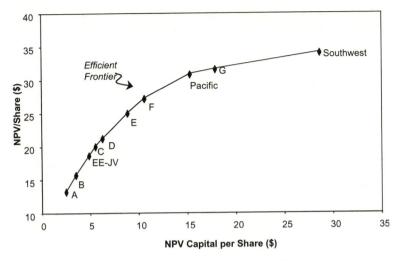

Figure 8.4 ChemTek's efficient frontier with acquisitions.

ure 8.4. The two new acquisition candidates are both up on the efficient frontier with the best of the company's internal alternatives, and far superior to Southwest Chemical.

Price Risk Balancing

Given the previous analysis, an executive team might feel that it has all the information it needs to make a high-quality decision. If no other alternatives were available to ChemTek, the acquisition of Southwest Chemical would improve the company's situation. Once some real alternatives are placed on the table, it is clear that ChemTek has much more productive uses for its limited capital. In fact, Southwest should be at the end of the pecking order of alternatives to pursue.

The analysis is incomplete, however, if the CEO fails to consider the risk balancing that these alternative portfolio strategies would provide or fail to pro-vide to ChemTek. Recall that ChemTek is a fairly un-balanced company—unbalanced in the sense that most of its assets are tied up in unstream businesses that produce raw materials and the primary chemical. Far fewer of its productive assets are involved in the downstream part of the chemical business—that is, very little of its business is involved with using those upstream products as ingredients in the making of value-added products, such as polymers.

Given the imbalance in its current strategy, Chem-Tek faces important primary chemcial price risks. When the market prices of raw materials and the pri-mary chemical are weak, the bulk of the company's business experiences low revenues. Those weak prices are good for the downstream, value-adding business because their input prices are low. However, because those value-adding businesses are small relative to the upstream business, low prices have a high negative effect on the overall revenues of the company. If this imbalance between upstream and downstream busi-nesses could be strategically reduced, price changes would have a much smaller impact on the earnings of the corporation as a whole—that is, ChemTek would be less vulnerable to price changes (primary-chemical price risk).

As shown in Figure 8.5. ChemTek's strategy to dou-ble its shareholder value by pursuing portfolio strategy F does not provide full risk balancing. Therefore, it may be too soon to say no to the Southwest Chemical acqui-sition. Buying it would clearly beef up the downstream side of ChemTek's business, making it less vulnerable to low raw-material and primary-chemical prices. The EEJV will also increase ChemTek's downstream pres-ence while Pacific is an upstream company. However,

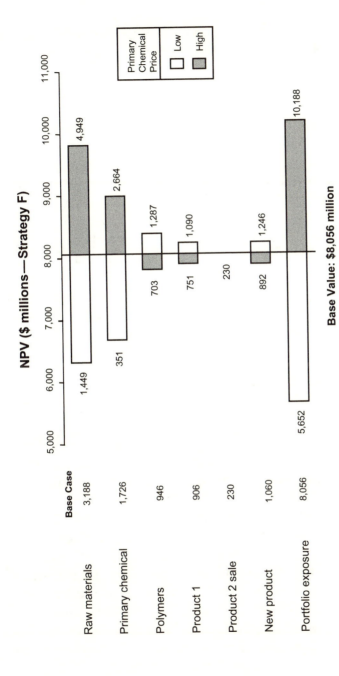

Figure 8.5 ChemTek's exposure to primary-chemical price with portfolio strategy F.

would Southwest's risk reduction in itself create value for shareholders? Many successful companies in highly cyclical industries have consciously elected not to balance their risks. Figure 8.5 helps answer this important question. It indicates that pursuit of strategy F would expose the portfolio as a whole to a major beating when primary chemical prices were low.

Figure 8.6 indicates ChemTek's exposure to primary-chemical price when it includes the two acquisitions, that decrease exposure to primary-chemical price—EE-JV and Southwest. It shows that having Southwest in the portfolio offsets some primary-chemical price risk. On the low end, the range from the base value is cut by about a third. Management must judge whether reducing overall risk by having Southwest Chemical in the portfolio is worth the trouble and huge balance-sheet implications.

Financial Policy

One final issue must be addressed before one can finally answer the question of whether an acquisition adds value for shareholders. That issue is the method of financing. A substantial body of literature indicates that acquisitions financed with the acquirer's stock—and not cash—are the most likely to fail.[5] Why is this the case? Perhaps cash buyers are simply more careful and rigorous in their selection methods.

Whatever the reason, acquirers should remember that a successful acquisition will increase the value of their shares. Thus, if they must pay $100 million for an acquisition—either in cash or stock—they should pause and reflect. If they pay with cash today, they know that their cost will be exactly $100 million. But if

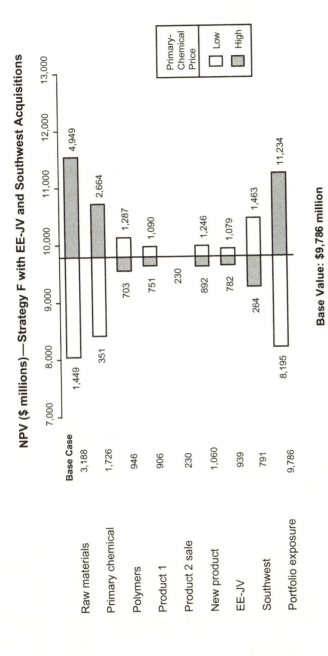

Figure 8.6 ChemTek's exposure to primary-chemical price with acquisitions.

this acquisition adds substantially to the company's future share value, paying with $100 million worth of today's shares means that they will be handing over shares worth much more than $100 million tomorrow. In effect, they will be giving away part of the upside prospects of their company. If analysis indicates, for example, that an acquisition strategy will increase the share price from $20 to $28 over the course of a year, would you rather give to owners of the target company $20 in cash or one share of your stock, which will soon be worth $28? If you are smart, you'll give them the cash and keep the upside profit in the stock as compensation for your good business sense and as a reward for your entrepreneurial work.

ALTERNATIVES ARE THE KEY

This chapters illustrates once again that a vigorous effort to identify and evaluate alternatives is the key to creating greater shareholder wealth. This is true whether a company seeks growth from within or from external acquisitions. The ChemTek case, a disguised version of a real company, is typical of what I regularly see in my consulting experiences. The great majority of companies suboptimize their value-creating performance, something they never realize until they've made concerted efforts to find alternatives to their current portfolio strategies. The record shows that most fall short when they seek growth through acquisitions. Business portfolios can be strengthened through acquisition, as this chapter has demonstrated, but only when the merits of acquisition candidates are compared with a full set of internal alternatives and found to be superior.

9

Managing through a Strategic Agenda

A portfolio company may be the ultimate challenge of an executive's ability to lead and manage. As seen in earlier chapters, different units of the same corporation may have very different success templates for creating value. They may also be at different stages of their business life cycles. The personnel who naturally gravitate to these units are likely to be temperamentally different and have different skills and expectations. Unfortunately, the annual routine of strategic planning does not help the executive in meeting this challenge. All of the old conglomerates did strategic planning in detail, yet all failed to realize their potential. Annual planning is better at producing recommendations than the good alternatives that executives and corporations need to succeed. And making the corporate plan the sum of individual unit plans practically guarantees performance *below* the efficient frontier.

Consider a hypothetical company, XYZ Corporation, with four operating units. Unit A is a mature, low-growth operation that produces a large, steady flow of cash for the corporate coffers. Because its products are fairly standard, success depends on its being an efficient, low-cost producer—which it has been for many years. Employees of Unit A are not particularly creative, but they are competent, efficient, and zealous in trimming costs and speeding shipments. Unit A runs like a Swiss watch.

Unit B is a very different creature. The key to its success has been its ability to continually innovate, render current products obsolete (including its own), and charge premium prices. Unit B's managers, engineers, and design personnel wear faded blue jeans and don't keep regular hours. Their offices are littered with pizza cartons and half-empty soda bottles. Yet to the amazement of the buttoned-down people at corporate headquarters, this small unit is highly profitable and growing rapidly. Customers use the term *awesome* when describing the innovative products designed and manufactured by Unit B.

On the other side of the country, Unit C is sputtering along like an old car with two bad cylinders and lousy compression. This once-vibrant business has lost market momentum during each of the past three years. Its former market dominance has been eclipsed by a new competitor, which has introduced a new technical standard that a growing number of customers favor. Profits for Unit C are getting more and more anemic, despite two rounds of layoffs. The strategy that kept this unit growing in the past has clearly lost its power.

Unit D came under the scrutiny of top management two years earlier, when its rate of sales growth began to sputter. After several years of double-digit sales growth, 2 to 3 percent year-over-year increases have become the norm. Alert corporate executives worked with Unit D managers and staff to develop a new strategy of customer engagement and new product development. All believed that this was the best approach to reinvigorating the unit. On paper, Unit D's new strategy should have returned it to prosperity, but after two full years, sales growth remained anemic. "It's our sales force," the unit's general manager complained, "They haven't gotten behind the program. Instead of engaging our customers and finding opportunities for products, they're still acting like order takers." Analysis confirmed the general manager's assessment.

With units like A, B, C, and D operating under the same umbrella, it is little wonder that corporate executives find leading and managing portfolio companies so difficult. Each business unit is unique; each has its own capabilities, mix of customers, competitive pressures, and people problems. Perhaps this is why so many CEOs try to manage by the numbers, set uniform goals for all units, put everyone through the wasteful process of annual strategic planning and replanning, and buy and sell operating units like shares in a stock portfolio.

There is a better way. Company executives can lead and manage the portfolio and individual units through a simple framework we called the *strategic agenda*.

The Strategic Agenda

The strategic agenda is a three-dimensional approach to managing:

1. Strategy development.
2. Implementation and change management.
3. Operations management.

The skills required to operate in these dimensions are quite different, particular with respect to the polar extremes. Operations management is inherently short term and action oriented, whereas strategy development requires a long-term view. Operations is also focused on detail and follow-through, whereas strategy development requires quick identification of the most important value-creation issues. A good operational manager often views alternatives and uncertainty as impediments to action—items that should be swept under the rug in the interest of getting going. These elements represent three levers that managers can use to control and direct businesses in the portfolio.

The first dimension is *strategy development,* which is motivated by this straightforward question:

> *What are the best strategies that our corporation and portfolio companies can pursue?* The best strategies are those that will put the corporation on its efficient frontiers, where it can produce the greatest shareholder value. Previous chapters have explained how this can be accomplished.

Once the best strategy for each portfolio unit has been identified, another question naturally rises to the surface:

How can we get people to accept and successfully implement the strategy? This dimension of the agenda is called *implementation and change management.* Implementation involves new business processes, tasks, and infrastructure; change management involves people's skills, culture, and behaviors.

When implementation is successful, there is one final question:

How can portfolio units continuously improve the execution of their chosen strategies. The term *operations management* describes this dimension of the strategy agenda. All else being equal, the business that continually improves its operations will outpace its competitors—at least until its current strategy runs out of steam.

The following sections consider each dimension of the strategic agenda in more detail.

Strategy Development

Strategy development is the first dimension of the agenda. Its goal is to find the best road for the corporation and its individual business units to follow—one that will put each on the corporate efficient frontiers (net income, capital, and risk). It looks at the current strategies being pursued by portfolio units, identifies those that are weak or underachieving, and helps those units develop higher-value strategies within the context of feasible alternatives. Unlike the corporate make-over approach of traditional strategic planning, strategy development focuses only on units that need a new strategy, and only when they need it. The result is less disruption to operations and lower costs.

Implementation and Change Management

Once the right road has been selected for a business, that business unit must get on it. Implementation and change management are the set of activities that makes this possible. They aim to implement the selected strategy in ways that realize its full value.

It is one thing to analyze the current business, find and evaluate alternatives, and do all the other things described in earlier chapters. Most of this is headwork—what is called strategic thinking. Getting people to *change* what they are doing and move in another direction is another—and often more difficult—matter. In some cases, business processes must be redesigned; in others, new infrastructure (distribution channels, manufacturing plants, information systems, etc.) may be needed. Compensation plans may be needed to align the interests of employees with the success of the new strategy. People must also change. They need to understand the logic and importance of the new strategy and must adopt its ends as their own. Often, employees need new skills to implement the strategy.

Effective implementation and change management require excellence in project management, training, organizational learning, and adaptation.

Operations Management

The focus of operations management is on activities designed to improve the value of the business unit and its current strategy. It is about getting better and better at what you are currently doing—that is, running faster and better along the road you are on. Running faster and better is an absolute requirement for success—no matter what the strategy. During the 1970s, for example, dozens of companies jumped into the minicomputer business. Most failed because they lacked the operational capabilities needed to compete, especially because customer support, software/applications, and price were key issues for customers.

Good operations management involves high-quality annual planning, excellent execution, accurate measurement, continuous improvement, and the setting of annual goals and budgets. The quality movement is in the domain of operations management. The decision to adopt an organizationwide quality program is strategic, and implementation is a massive change-management effort. However, once the quality program is in place, it becomes just another element of good operations management, improving productivity and meeting customer expectations through continuous improvement.

The big danger of continual operational improvement is that it can make a company dangerously myopic. Self-absorption with operational elegance creates the risk of getting better and better at things that have no future. What company, for example, wants to be the world's most efficient producer of vacuum tubes, vinyl records, or buggy whips? None. Fortunately, with strategy development as part of the three-dimensional agenda, this risk can be eliminated.

Setting the Strategic Agenda

Figure 9.1 illustrates a framework for setting the strategic agenda. Identifying the strategic agenda means

Figure 9.1 The strategic-agenda framework.

identifying timely strategy development, change management, and operations management needs and goals. Most companies that operate successfully with a strategy agenda do this every year. "Timely" implies that the agenda item should be addressed in the coming year. This is not to say that a company should *re-strategize* annually. Far from it. Each of the portfolio businesses is examined annually in terms of the agenda's three dimensions. Three questions identify issues that should become part of the year's strategic agenda:

1. Is the business unit following the best strategy for creating value?
2. If it has the right strategy, is the unit successfully implementing it?
3. If it has successfully implemented the right strategy, is the unit getting more and more effective in its operations?

For example, Unit A of our hypothetical XYZ Corporation is slow growing under its current strategy but throws off lots of cash. Operationally, it is highly tuned and continually getting better. Does Unit A need a new strategy? This should be debated. A good case could be made for leaving it alone. It is a good business, but if there are potential opportunities to increase growth, or if new trends threaten the current strategy, then the CEO might ask a team to begin a deliberate search for alternatives to the unit's current strategy. This search would become an item for the year's strategic agenda. If no new strategy is needed this year, then neither is change management. In terms of operations management, Unit A seems to be doing extremely well and an operations agenda, including goals and budget guidelines, should be set to reinforce continuous improvement.

Over in Unit B, continual product innovation by its team of blue-jeaned wunderkinds appears to be working extremely well. Neither new strategy nor change management appear to be necessary. However, Unit B might benefit from a dose of the operational excellence exhibited by Unit A. Great new products may cause the cash register to ring, but in the end, the unit needs efficiency and excellence in manufacturing and service to keep it ringing and to improve profitability. Operations management at Unit B could be an item for this year's strategic agenda, perhaps addressed by a team drawn from Units A and B.

Unit C, in contrast to its sister units, is in real trouble. Its success template has clearly run out of steam. A full course of strategy development should be on the agenda, guided by a dialogue process similar to that described in Chapter 2. Using this process, the corporation's executive team should charter a working group of corporate staff and Unit C managers to do the following:

- Assess Unit C's current business strategy.
- Develop a set of alternative strategies.
- Evaluate the risk/return aspects of those alternatives.

The executive team would then decide which represents the best strategy and instruct the working group to develop a plan of action for implementation. This is a big job, but experience indicates that it is more efficient and effective than the traditional nostrum of making every unit jump through the same set of standard hoops.

Unit D already *has* a new strategy but has failed to implement it. Implementation failure is often evidence of people problems. And sure enough, Unit D's salespeople have not changed from being order takers to becoming the proactive sales-and-marketing people required by the strategy. For this unit, a dose of change management is in order. Depending on the true source of the problem, Unit D's salespeople may need to do one or more of the following:

- Understand the strategy and their place in it (perhaps no one has bothered to do this).
- Receive training on building customer relationships.
- Understand how they can integrate their customer insights into the product-development program required by the strategy.

In addition, change management within Unit D may call for a reassessment of the existing incentive system. The interests of sales-force personnel must be aligned with the aims of the new strategy.

Developing a Strategic Agenda

It is always better to do a few important things well than to handle many things in a second-rate manner. This commonplace wisdom applies equally to the strategic agenda. If the corporation is not selective about what becomes part of the strategic agenda, the talent and energy of its problem solvers and implementers will be dissipated. The strategic agenda should be limited to items that do the following:

- Affect long-term shareholder value.
- Require major change in the way the corporation or a business unit operates.
- Have a significant effect on the cost of doing business.
- Are timely.
- Set key goals for the corporation, a business, or a major function for the coming year.

Corporations typically identify strategic-agenda items by scanning internally and externally for opportunities, problems, and threats. The biggest challenge in doing this is external scanning. Most companies see the outside world through rose-colored glasses. They need a highly developed external perspective that is untainted by their own perspectives. Scanning requires an "outside-in perspective," as defined by Jim and David Matheson.[1] Here are a few examples of this external perspective in action:

- One manufacturer routinely asks its personnel, worldwide, to purchase and send to its corporate R&D lab a case of any new competing product they see on the shelf.
- Another company routinely evaluates its competitor's production costs, including new plants under construction.
- A pharmaceutical company evaluates all competitive products, including those in development.

Strategic issues that companies pick up in scanning are monitored periodically to determine if they should become strategic-agenda items. In most corporations, a small corporate staff coordinates scanning and monitoring.

Figure 9.2 illustrates a typical process flow for developing a strategic agenda. This process utilizes inputs from the business units as well as a corporate-level strategic planning council to identify potential items for the strategic agenda. The actual strategic agenda is developed at an annual meeting chaired by the CEO; this meeting includes business-unit and functional

Figure 9.2 Setting a strategic agenda.

heads. Setting the strategic agenda replaces the old annual corporate strategy meeting. The strategic-agenda meeting is a platform for the CEO to lead the corporation by setting the agenda for the coming year. His or her leadership, with input from others, defines the strategy goals, major change initiatives, and operation-budget guidelines that will drive the organization forward through the new year.

Once set, the strategic agenda is used to charter major strategy development, implementation and change management, and operational efforts for the coming year. In addition, the company uses the operational agenda to develop detailed budgeting guidelines and drive the budgeting process.

What the Best Companies Do

The strategic-agenda framework is designed as a mechanism for corporate leadership through which executives can implement the portfolio-management principles and methodologies described in previous chapters. But how realistic is this advice? Will it produce the desired results? To answer these questions, our firm benchmarked a number of outstanding companies. This study, conducted in 1997, aimed to identify best practices for strategic management. The 10 companies selected for study represented a range of industries: computers equipment, electronic equipment, software, pharmaceuticals, financial services, petroleum, chemicals, telecommunications, and entertainment. They represented a range of management styles and included both old and new companies. Revenues for these companies (in 1996) ranged between $8 billion and $40 billion. By just about any measure—

revenues, product/service innovation, market share, and so forth—these companies qualified as industry leaders. About half were clients of our firm; the rest were not. (This study was a qualitative, holistic analysis of strategic-planning systems. It concentrated on understanding the processes in use and rationales behind different process-design choices.) All were portfolio businesses; and 2 of the 10 were themselves units within an extremely large portfolio business. Although the focus of this study was the corporate aspects of strategic planning, the topic of business-unit planning arose repeatedly. Accordingly, the study identified some of the different ways in which corporate planning interfaces with business units.

Interviews with senior executives of the 10 companies revealed the use of a wide variety of strategic-management models. Nevertheless, the study revealed common patterns linking a company's choice of strategic-management approach to its culture, management style, or business environment. The benchmarking identified a number of best practices currently in use by all 10 companies:

- The companies conducted strategy development "as needed" and "where needed." Strategy development—including the consideration of alternatives—was initiated *only* when clearly needed for added growth or renewal.
- Each of the 10 companies made use of a strategic agenda to actively manage its business portfolio.
- Strategy development followed a process emphasizing dialogue with multiple meetings between the corporation and its business units and functions; companies supported this process with appropriate resources.

- Strategy development processes varied between companies from highly specific to ad hoc. For example, one company issued a 110-page process manual to its managers, detailing a step-by-step procedure for strategy development, but business units could customize the process and tools as appropriate. Other companies did not specify the process but did specify deliverables. Several companies issued a strategy template.

- All 10 companies made use of some form of strategic planning council (SPC). The CEO, chief operating officer, chief financial officer, and heads of the sectors or business units were almost always members of these councils, and the head of corporate planning often played the role of secretary. There was a range of levels of SPC engagement in the strategy process.

- Each of the companies engaged in some form of scanning and monitoring as inputs to developing its strategic agenda.

- These companies recognized differences between portfolio units—that is, they understood and accommodated the life cycles and unique success templates of portfolio units. The conglomerate management style of running them by the numbers was definitely out. Instead, all recognized the unique challenges faced by their different units. They also focused on understanding and measuring the value contributed by each portfolio business to the corporation.

- The companies actively sought alternatives to current strategy. Unfortunately, not all alternatives were evaluated.

- These companies dealt with risks objectively—that is, they recognized and assessed the risks using financial and nonfinancial measures. However, with the exception of oil, pharmaceutical, and electronics companies, which experience risk routinely, many of these companies made limited use of risk measurement. Those companies that quantitatively measured risk reported success and stated the desire to extend that practice more generally. All companies stated that the ability to measure risk would make it possible to incorporate risk in strategy development and to create an environment in which risk could be shared by the corporation and its individual business units. This environment, they stated, would encourage employees to surface and consider riskier but higher-value strategies. All companies studied identified risk measurement as an area for future improvement.

- The companies carefully linked resources and value-creating opportunities. Each company developed detailed financial projections for strategic plans and based operating and capital budgets on those projections.

SOME EXAMPLES

To see some of the principles just outlined at work, consider 4 of the 10 companies in the 1997 Navigant study. Each has a unique approach to strategy development, which is determined by its culture and the challenges that it faces. Although each company implements these practices in a way unique to its history and culture, the main themes appear everywhere. If there is a lesson, it is the following: Don't blindly imitate others; take the time to adapt the practices recommended here to your business, culture, and CEO.

Corporation A: Strategizing as Needed

One subject of the study was a leading U.S. financial-services corporation—one of the world's largest. Over the years, Corporation A has grown from being a major money-center bank to becoming a leader in consumer credit, retail banking, and lending on a global basis.

Corporation A has no permanent planning group at the corporate level. Instead, it creates a planning group as strategic needs require and disbands it when no strategy-development items are on the agenda. It creates special teams as needed to develop strategy and address implementation/change items on the agenda. It can operate this way, in part, because top-level executives are good strategic thinkers; they do not need a dedicated planning group to continuously scan for new strategic issues. Instead, senior executives identify new strategic agenda items in the course of their other duties.

Overall, Corporation A follows a top-down process of strategic planning. However, the business units play an important part in the total process, and "share-of-mind" sessions communicate strategies and visions down the organization. Bottom-up planning occurs within the business units and is discussed with the senior management team via dialogue; strategic issues regarding the businesses are also monitored at the business level. Some business-unit functions, such as market development or product development, may feed into planning. The corporation also looks to its business-unit managers to design strategy for their own units.

Many believe that this enterprise has succeeded because of its ability to adopt and implement the latest information technology and to identify emerging markets. In effect, this is a process of seeking out alternatives. The study found that these alternatives and their risks were analyzed or evaluated quantitatively at the business-unit level.

Being a top-down strategizer, Corporation A leaves the final say to its CEO. It then looks to its business-unit managers for implementation; it uses performance measures to align the activities of these unit managers with the intentions of strategy.

Although this corporation enjoys a great deal of success, it relies heavily on the ability of its senior executives to identify strategic issues and opportunities. This risk is mitigated to the extent that its strategic process provides opportunities for others, particularly in the business units, to contribute.

Corporation B: Decentralized Decision Making

Corporation B is one of the world's foremost and respected electronics companies. Like many great enterprises, its power rests on the inventiveness and business acumen of its operating divisions, which, in this case, are given a great deal of autonomy. That autonomy has led some observers to describe this company as more "confederate" than corporate. Nevertheless, a culture of collaboration keeps this world-beating business from becoming a battleground of warring fiefdoms. The company's CEO facilitates this culture by acting as a catalyst for cross-business synergy and collaboration.

In line with its tradition of decentralization, strategy development within Corporation B is largely conducted at the operating-unit level, the units being encouraged to strategize as they wish, with the division managers generally having the ultimate decision-making power. Interdivision and intergroup teams are brought together to handle special initiatives. A common process for addressing strategic issues adds cohesion to these efforts. The corporate level encourages strategy development by the business units and provides education on the use of a common set of processes and tools. The process itself has shown itself to be effective both in surfacing and evaluating new opportunities and, because it harnesses input from many people throughout the organization, in generating commitment to eventual strategy implementation.

The corporation routinely evaluates alternative strategies found within its existing businesses, using scenario analysis. However, the study found no evidence that the company routinely scans beyond its existing businesses for opportunities. The level of analysis is more qualitative than quantitative at Corporation B, and it does not systematically account for risk.

Once a new direction is chosen, this corporation is first-rate at getting people and their activities on board, using measurable goals and a staff of change-management personnel for that purpose.

Corporation C: Dialogue and Analysis

Corporation C is a major player in the consumer-products industry, both in North America and overseas. Unlike the first two corporations, strategy planning in Corporation C is neither top-down nor bottom-up but is based on balanced dialogue between headquarters and its operating units. Lean strategic planning and business-development functions are shared and found at both the corporate level and within geographic units (e.g., Latin America and Europe).

There are, in fact, three planning staffs operating with the same structure, and all report to the CFO.

Senior corporate management sets the strategic agenda in this organization, and corporate finance provides financial forecasting and budget updating based on inputs made by operating units. However, portfolio units are actively engaged in forming strategy, both for the corporation and for themselves.

Perhaps more than at any other company in this study, Corporation C stresses the importance of actively seeking alternatives to its current strategies. Furthermore, it subjects these alternatives to rigorous analysis and even provides employees with a manual describing decision-analysis and risk-assessment methods. The company's faith in quantitative measures is further indicated by its regular use of NPV and EVA.

Corporation D: No Barriers to Strategic Input

The study found the greatest attempt to open the strategic planning effort to all—senior management, business units, and rank-and-file employees alike—at a highly successful software company, one noted for its relentless pursuit of future opportunities. Senior management at Corporation D is highly strategic, yet it encourages open participation in the planning process. In theory, anyone can jump into the game;

many do, firing off e-mails to the corporate chairman as they spot new opportunities.

Environmental scanning occurs in all areas and at all levels of this organization, and dialogue between different parts and levels of the organization is widespread. This creates a wellspring of observations and ideas, most of which are put forward by the business units.

Given the intensely future orientation of Corporation D, its many levels of strategic-planning staffing is not surprising. Two- or three-person planning staffs work within each business unit (nearly 200 people in total). Another 10 staffers work at the corporate level in business development.

Perhaps owing to the emerging nature of the software industry, this company takes a fairly qualitative approach to considering data and opportunity alternatives. It also relies on the ability of its leaders, and especially the founder-chairman, to transform raw information into strategic business concepts. The founder-chairman takes periodic retreats for this purpose.

The great strategic challenge for Corporation D is to keep ahead of competitors in the fast-evolving field of computers, software, and networking. Its ability to identify and implement good strategic alternatives will determine its future.

A PRACTICAL TOOL

For executives who are tired of fruitless strategic planning and puzzled by the complexities of portfolio companies with different characteristics, the strategic agenda described in this chapter represents a practical tool for managing and leading change. If you handle each of its elements well, you will have done all that any senior executive could be asked to do, namely:

- Identify best strategies that your corporation and its units can pursue.
- Get people to accept and successfully implement the strategy.
- Improve strategy execution through excellence in operations management.

Get these right, and the rest will fall into place.

10

Toward Better Management of Portfolio Companies

An entire generation of executives has come and gone since the heyday of the conglomerate kings. That empire-building era, which was often undisciplined and driven by hubris and chutzpah, has largely passed into history. In the years since, many executives have become more sophisticated in their approach to managing portfolio corporations and their individual units. They have learned that they cannot sustain growth in shareholder wealth simply by cabling together unrelated businesses with the right financial characteristics; instead, they must nurture and grow the businesses in their portfolios. Nor can they sustain growth by playing fund manager from the isolation of the executive suite, trading slow-growing units for more promising ones like so many stock positions. The by-the-numbers approach of the late Harold Geneen is likewise understood to be insufficient. Each of these approaches fails to come to grips with the foundation upon which value creation is based:

- Creative strategic alternatives.
- Knowledge of how each alternative will create value and how much value will be created.
- A clear understanding of the risks.

In the absence of this foundation, even the most elaborately crafted strategies will fail. And the cost of failure is high: Shareholder value suffers, bonuses evaporate, morale declines, and heads roll. What's needed instead is an active and intelligent system for guiding each portfolio unit to its maximum potential.

The potential for creating shareholder value through portfolios of operating businesses remains unlimited. Today, multibusiness corporations are the leaders in virtually every major industry. Some of the major portfolio companies of the conglomerate era — General Electric, Merck, Pfizer, Procter & Gamble, Coca-Cola, Hewlett-Packard, Motorola, and Citigroup to name just a few — are successful portfolio companies today. All these companies have focused on surfacing the best internal alternatives while continuously reshaping their portfolios as conditions change. As a result, they continue to be major players in their industries.

The best-practice companies clearly operate with the right tools and methods: They insist on alternatives, they understand the potential of different strategies to create shareholder value, and they are straightforward in dealing with risk. All follow a process for strategy development and decision making similar to the dialogue process described in Chapter 2. They also operate with a strategy agenda.

If these leading portfolio companies can accomplish these feats, so can yours, and the principles and methods described in the preceding chapters can get you started. They are restated here as action steps:

• *Identify the efficient frontier for your organization and do what you need to do to reach it.* A portfolio is efficient to the extent that it maximizes shareholder value relative to other parameters, such as risk, capital investment, or short-term earnings. An efficient frontier indicates the optimal set of portfolio choices available to any given company. Where you stand relative to the efficient frontier indicates the efficiency of your portfolio of businesses. All new strategic initiatives and acquisitions should be judged in terms of this question: Will they improve your efficient frontier?

• *Expand the frontier by means of creative alternatives.* The efficient frontier is not static—it can be continually expanded as new opportunities appear. The focus of the CEO's strategic agenda should be on both reaching the frontier and pushing it to higher levels. The best way to do this is to develop a culture that fosters the development of high-value ideas and alternatives. Implement incentives to encourage creative alternatives and offer risky alternatives. Eliminate incentive systems that discourage value-creating alternatives and prudent risk taking.

• *Adopt a structured dialogue process for developing alternatives and choosing among them.* Process has been emphasized throughout this book, with special attention given to a dialogue process for making better decisions about business-unit and portfolio strategy.

This process can become the glue that binds together the modern corporation, its personnel, and its many disparate activities. It is the basis for trust within the organization, and it assures management at all levels that all feasible alternatives are being surfaced and evaluated. It creates a climate in which executives can pursue risky value-creating alternatives with confidence, knowing that the risks are understood and shared by the entire organization. Decisions in this process are made through dialogue between high-level executives, who have the authority to allocate resources, and the personnel who are closest to markets and the businesses under scrutiny. The dialogue process is emerging as a best practice for creating and evaluating alternatives, and it can help your organization.

• *Don't sweep risk under the rug-measure it, share it, and engage it directly.* Risk is the handmaiden of all progress and value creation. If your company is not stepping up to a reasonable level of risk, it is not doing its job on behalf of shareholders. The first step in dealing with risk is *measurement.* As Lord Kelvin said: "When you can measure what you are speaking about and express it in numbers, you know something about it; but when you cannot measure it...your knowledge is of a meager and unsatisfactory kind."

Once risk has been measured, discuss the risk in current and proposed operations openly. Deal with risk objectively and avoid recriminations when people take well-calculated risks that backfire. Create a climate in which employees can and will pursue risky opportunities that clearly benefit shareholders.

• *Align incentives for value creation.* Be sure that your incentive system supports and encourages value creation including development of high value alternatives.

To do this, identify the sources of value creation using the analytic methods described throughout this book, then align incentives with those sources. For example, if your business is at the point in its life cycle where its success template has lost its power, give people incentives to find a new and more powerful one.

• *Every profitable portfolio corporation has at most a handful of success templates Many have only one. Understand your success template and manage it for all its worth. Recognize when you need to strengthen or abandon it in favor of another.* Every successful business has a mechanism for sustaining market power and profitability. What is yours? Whatever it is, make sure that employees understand and nurture it. Use that template as a standard against which to judge the compatibility of potential new businesses (i.e., internal initiatives, external acquisitions, etc.) Remember, too, that different portfolio units may operate under different success templates. If this is the case in your company, recognize these differences and don't make the mistake of trying to manage all units in the same way.

Nothing lasts forever, including the template that accounts for your current success. Be willing and able to abandon it and adopt a new one when its market power begins to slip away. Use your portfolio strategy to leverage, strengthen, and evolve your success template. Success templates can be leveraged and strengthened through acquisitions.

• *Understand the life cycle of each business in your portfolio, then try to identify where each is situated in that cycle.* The businesses in your portfolio are most likely at different points in their natural life cycles, which are (1) business R&D, (2) emerging, (3) established, and (4) challenged. Manage them accordingly. If you find one business in the business R&D phase, look for a success template with the potential to make it a leader. If another is in the emerging phase, put the pedal to the floor and take as much market share as possible. Businesses in the established phase should be managed to capture as much value as possible even as a path for renewal is sought. Finally, any business in the challenged phase must find a new template for success or be prepared to wither on the vine.

• *Use the concept of EVA to project and track the value contribution of each unit over time.* Standard accounting measures give a false picture of value creation, yet a surprising number of businesspeople continue to use them in making strategic decisions. Don't be one of them. Instead, operate with measures that indicate real economic value and how your stock is likely to respond as you create value. Build shareholder expectations around EVA, and manage to those expectations. Avoid ratio measures including those based on EVA.

• *Treat an acquisition candidate as you would any other strategic alternative.* Evaluate each acquisition candidate in terms of its potential to improve the efficient frontier. You can apply the methods described in this book for analyzing internally generated alternatives to the analysis of acquisition candidates. Use these methods to determine how an acquisition would (like any other alternative) reposition your company relative to its efficient frontier.

• *Understand the acquisition candidate's success template and then use your success template to judge each acquisition's fit with your corporation.* Beware of acquisition candidates that have radically different success templates. Ask if you and your team can really add value to a business with a very different success template. At the same time recognize that an acquisition candidate can leverage and strengthen your success template.

- *Throw your annual strategic-planning books into the trash. Lead, instead, through a strategic agenda.* Most annual planning regimes are time wasters and do little to help the CEO to lead and renew the corporation. Instead, guide your organization through the three-dimensional approach offered in Chapter 9: strategy development, implementation, and operational management. Even as you lead the corporation in following its strategic agenda, anticipate next year's challenges. Enrich those challenges through scanning and monitoring.
- *Use the strategic agenda and portfolio strategy to drive budgets.* Because portfolio strategy is selected based on the efficient frontiers, you should use the portfolio strategy to drive both the operating and capital budgets. Portfolio strategy is the allocation of expense and capital resources. Don't reverse the portfolio strategy during the budget process.

These action steps will help you optimize the performance of your business portfolio. The end result will be greater value for shareholders and more rewards and opportunities for managers and employees.

Notes

Chapter 1

[1] Robert Sobel, *The Rise and Fall of the Conglomerate Kings* (New York: Stein and Day, 1984), 139.

[2] From *Dun's Review,* November 1965, as described in *International Telephone & Telegraph Corp. (A),* Harvard Business School Case 9-472-007, revised October 3, 1994 (Boston, MA: Harvard Business School Press, 1994), 21.

[3] Michael E. Porter, "From Competitive Advantage to Corporate Strategy," *Harvard Business Review,* May–June 1987, 3.

[4] Noel Tichy and Ram Charan, "Speed, Simplicity, Self-Confidence: An Interview with Jack Welch," *Harvard Business Review,* September–October 1989, 114.

[5] ITT's telecommunications business, which accounted for approximately 30 percent of consolidated revenues, was sold in 1986 to form Alcatel, a joint venture with France's Compagnie Générale d'Electricité.

[6]*Corning Glass Works, International (A),* Harvard Business School Case 9-3-79-051 (Boston, MA: Harvard Business School Press, 1978).

[7]Lewis Berman, "What We Learned from the Great Merger Frenzy," *Fortune,* April 1973, 70–144.

[8]Harry M. Markowitz, "Portfolio Selection," *Journal of Finance,* March 1952, 77–91.

[9]Stern and Stewart created the concept of EVA. See G. Bennett Stewart, *The Quest for Value* (New York: HarperBusiness, 1991), 118–178. Economic Value Added is a trademark of the Stern Stuart Consulting Company.

Chapter 2

[1]Sumantra Ghoshal and Christopher A. Bartlett, "Changing the Role of Top Management: Beyond Structure to Process," *Harvard Business Review,* January–February 1995, 86–96.

[2]Jim Matheson and David Matheson, *The Smart Organization* (Boston, MA: Harvard Business School Press, 1998).

Chapter 3

[1]Christopher Bartlett and Sumantra Ghoshal, "Beyond Strategic Planning to Organizational Learning: Lifeblood of the Individualized Corporation," *Strategy and Leadership,* January–February 1998, 34–39.

[2]Robert Alexander and Douglas Smith, *Fumbling the Future: How Xerox Invented, then Ignored, the First Personal Computer* (New York: William Morrow, 1988).

[3]David Matheson and Jim Matheson, *Strategic Risk—Get Smart* (Menlo Park, CA: Strategic Decisions Group, 1998), 2.

Chapter 4

[1]This case derives from the experience of Carl Spetzler and a team of Navigant consultants. It was originally told by Jim Math-

eson and David Matheson in *The Smart Organization* (Boston, MA: Harvard Business School Press, 1998), 102–105. My thanks to them and to the publisher for permission to repeat the case and figures here.

[2] Sumantra Ghoshal and Christopher A. Bartlett, *The Individualized Corporation* (New York: HarperBusiness, 1997).

[3] For example, see Vince Barabba, *Meeting of the Minds* (Boston, MA: Harvard Business Press, 1995).

[4] For example, see Paul Sharpe and Tom Keelin, "How Smith-Kline Beecham Makes Better Resource Allocation Decisions," *Harvard Business Review*, March–April, 1998.

[5] This is the approach recommended by the creators of EVA, Joel Stern and Bennett Stewart.

[6] Edward De Bono, *Serious Creativity: Using the Power of Lateral Thinking to Create New Ideas* (New York: HarperBusiness, 1992).

[7] Robert Friedel and Paul Israel, *Edison's Electric Light: Biography of an Invention* (New Brunswick, NJ: Rutgers University Press, 1986), 13–14.

[8] Cited in Friedel and Israel, Edison's *Electric Light*, xii.

Chapter 5

[1] See G. Bennett Stewart, *The Quest for Value* (New York: HarperBusiness, 1991).

[2] See, for example, Richard A. Brealey and Stewart C. Myers, *Principles of Corporate Finance* (New York: McGraw-Hill, 1996).

[3] *Standard & Poor's Analysts' Handbook: 1998 Annual Edition* (New York: McGraw-Hill, 1998), 245.

[4] William Taylor, "Message and Muscle: An Interview with Swatch Titan Nicolas Hayek," *Harvard Business Review*, March–April 1993; 103.

[5] *Hewlett-Packard: Company Report*, June 7, 1996; (New York: Salomon Brothers, 1996), 9–10.

Chapter 6

[1] The concept of core competency was created by C.K. Prahalad and Gary Hamel. See Gary Hamel and C.K. Prahalad, *Com-*

peting for the Future (Boston, MA: Harvard Business School Press, 1995).

[2]Joan Magretta, "The Power of Virtual Integration: An Interview with Dell Computer's Michael Dell," *Harvard Business Review,* March–April 1998, 73–84.

[3]Leo Reynolds, "The History of the Microwave Oven," *Microwave World,* Summer 1995.

[4]James M. Utterback, *Mastering the Dynamics of Innovation* (Boston, MA: Harvard Business School Press, 1994), 169.

[5]From a letter by George Eastman, cited in Utterback, *Mastering the Dynamics,* 173.

[6]Helmut Gernsheim, *A Concise History of Photography* (New York: Grosset and Dunlop, 1965), 36.

[7]Geoffrey Smith, "Can George Fisher Fix Kodak?" *Business Week,* October 20, 1997, 116.

Chapter 7

[1]Richard Preston has captured this period of steel-making history, and the rise of Nucor, in *American Steel* (New York: Prentice Hall, 1991).

[2]Mary Ann Keller describes GM's situation and Chapter 10 describes the automation investments in *Rude Awakening* (William Morrow and Company, 1989).

Chapter 8

[1]Alexandra Reed Lajoux and J. Fred Weston, "Do Deals Deliver on Postmerger Performance?" *Mergers and Acquisitions,* September–October 1998, 34.

[2]Phillip L. Zweig, Judy Pearlman Klein, and Kevin Gudridge, "The Case against Mergers," *BusinessWeek,* October 30, 1995, 122.

[3]Dwight Gertz and João Baptista, *Grow to Be Great* (New York: Free Press, 1996), 31–43.

[4]"Chairman's Letter," in *Berkshire Hathaway Annual Report,* 1981, 2–3.

[5]Tim Loughran and Anand M. Fijh, "Do Long-Term Shareholders Benefit from Corporate Acquisitions?" *Journal of Finance,* December 1997, 1765–1790.

Chapter 9

[1]Jim Matheson and David Matheson, *The Smart Organization* (Boston, MA: Harvard Business School Press, 1998), 133–135.

[2]This Navigant Consulting study was a qualitative, holistic analysis of strategic planning systems. It concentrated on understanding the processes in use and rationales behind different process-design choices.

Index